Evaluating Early Years Practice in Your School

A practical tool for reflective teaching

Ann Langston

FEATHERSTONE

LONDON   OXFORD   NEW YORK   NEW DELHI   SYDNEY

FEATHERSTONE
Bloomsbury Publishing Plc
50 Bedford Square, London, WC1B 3DP, UK

BLOOMSBURY, FEATHERSTONE and the Feather logo are trademarks of Bloomsbury Publishing Plc

First published in Great Britain, 2019

A catalogue record for this book is available from the British Library

ISBN: PB: 978-1-4729-5916-4; ePDF: 978-1-4729-5918-8; ePub: 978-1-4729-5914-0

2 4 6 8 10 9 7 5 3 1

Typeset by Newgen KnowledgeWorks Pvt. Ltd., Chennai, India
Printed and bound by CPI Group (UK) Ltd, Croydon CR0 4YY

To find out more about our authors and books visit www.bloomsbury.com
and sign up for our newsletters

Contents

Online resources accompanying this book at: www.bloomsbury.com/evaluating-EY-practice-in-schools.

Please type the URL into your web browser and follow the instructions to access the resources. If you experience any problems, please contact Bloomsbury at companionwebsite@bloomsbury.com.

Foreword

The EYFS is an educational phase where teachers sometimes feel they plough a lonely furrow because few others in the school share their experience of working with three- to five-year-olds – children whose take on the world is unique and who are still developing emotionally, socially, linguistically and physically. Because of this there are few points of comparison with provision and practice in other parts of the school and the result is that teachers in the EYFS often feel isolated especially when Ofsted inspections occur because the EYFS is given a separate rating to the rest of the school. With this in mind I am often invited by leaders to contribute to evaluation of the EYFS – a task I delight in because of the many committed and positive teachers I meet who are determined to get practice and provision right for the children in their school. When I visit schools, I am struck by the clarity of teachers in identifying their own issues – some structural such as only having an outdoor space that is not accessed directly from the classroom, others time-related such as the demands of maintaining an indoor and outdoor classroom effectively – tasks few others in the school face.

However, when schools offer time and support to teachers and school leaders (dependent on the size and numbers of classes in the EYFS) by inviting external evaluation, there are usually significant changes because teachers are able to engage in professional discussions about practice and make adjustments which support high-quality play and learning in the school.

When this transformation happens, there is usually a buzz in the air and the adults involved often describe a renewed sense of engagement which is palpable. As a result, adults and children seem to thrive and opportunities for learning increase.

The purpose behind this book is to share the thoughts and ideas that guide the thinking that occurs as I work with teachers in schools to evaluate practice. The main thing that emerges as we discuss the pros and cons of what we observe during typical sessions is the value of having another person give their perspective on issues as they emerge – some things then become immediately obvious, for example, we might think: if we moved the sound-making table into the outdoor area we could accommodate the role play area better. But some things take more time and many different attempts at altering them before a satisfactory outcome is reached.

If you are keen to engage in self-evaluation I hope that the many documents in this book will help you to stand back and see your learning environment through new eyes and that, in doing so, you will be able to find a way forward if you are intent on continuously developing your practice and provision.

Special thanks to the Learning Network of South Failsworth Primary School, SS Aidan & Oswald RC Primary School; St Edward's RC Primary School and Christ Church CE Primary

School, Oldham, especially for their Outdoor Learning Mission statement. Thanks also to Erica Mason (MrsM@Whitefieldhead) at Whitefield Infant School and Nursery, Nelson, Lancashire for her generosity in allowing me to visit her wonderful school and to share photographs of the school's splendid learning environment. My grateful thanks also to Erdington Hall Primary School, Birmingham and all those that have so generously taken time to share their ideas and read and give feedback on various drafts of this book, as well as all those who have allowed me to work with them and to share their stories – you inspire me every day and I think you are wonderful! Finally, this book is dedicated to my family, especially my grandchildren Sylvie and Teddy, with thanks for all their support.

1 Self-evaluation: Measuring the success of your provision

Key points

- Reflect on your practice to ensure that you maintain a fresh approach to teaching and learning
- Don't be afraid to ask for feedback from others – including colleagues, parents and children
- Act on feedback from peers and keep a record to show the steps you have taken to improve
- Self-evaluate so you can identify your strengths and any areas for development

Maintaining a fresh approach to teaching and learning

One of the most wonderful things about teaching young children is that whilst annually we may have to repeat some of the same things from year to year, we are still presented with a varying range of issues to deal with every day. And, the work is never predictable or dull because of the many children and adults we work with and the environment and resources we manage. Given this, maintaining a fresh approach to teaching and learning is relatively straightforward; however, without reflection on practice, it can be all too easy to drop a gear, adopting an automatic rather than a considered response to practice issues. To avoid this, it is important to reflect on what we are doing and why we are doing it.

Reflecting on what we do sometimes happens whilst we are doing it but more often occurs when we are away from the classroom when questions or ideas may flood our thoughts, such as: *'Should I have done x, or y?'* or *'Was that the right way to do z?'* All the time our minds busily replay different scenarios, intensifying feelings of uncertainty – some seeming far worse than the reality of what we actually did, or of what we think we might have got wrong! When this happens, our evaluations provide us with an opportunity to do things differently, saving us from the curse of what I think of as the 'hardy perennial' approach where, usually during periods of stress or extreme pressure, adults can fall back on doing what they have done previously. But, as we know, if you continue to do the same thing you will get the same result, so, although at these times the important thing is to survive, it is also important to try to change, once the crisis has passed. Ultimately, it is more helpful to become proactive so that in the future things never reach that point again.

Obtaining feedback

How can we maintain a fresh approach to teaching and learning? Well, obvious though it may sound seeking feedback from others – including colleagues, parents and children – is a great way of hearing good things about your practice, as well as of finding out about areas for improvement. An example of a reflective practitioner I often quote to teachers is a friend, who, having spent more than twenty years in the same school, still diligently went in to her classroom during the summer holidays to re-arrange it because she knew the needs of each cohort of children she taught always demanded a different layout to her classroom. Even when she retired she said she hadn't managed to get it right every time!

Ways of seeking feedback need to be simple and build in a guarantee of 'no-blame' – in other words they should be easy to complete and you shouldn't get upset or annoyed if one hundred per cent of the feedback isn't positive. Indeed, there will be a range of responses, some of which may please you, whilst some may not; nevertheless, your reaction to all feedback should be positive because ultimately somebody's honesty may be helping you to identify an area of your practice where you can improve!

A simple idea for feedback about practice could be achieved through providing 'smiley' stickers for parents or children to add to a display showing something children have worked on, such as making potions in a mud kitchen. Many responses will be positive and fill you full of pride as you judge the majority to be pleased with your input as the stickers mount in the 'Very happy' box. On the other hand, one or two parents might not have appreciated the fact that when this work was ongoing their children's T-shirts were covered in red dye and so may have placed a couple of lone 'sad' faces in the 'Not so happy' box. Even this should be considered 'good' feedback, since this can be filed in your brain under the heading: *Evaluation – what would I do differently next time?* Evaluating what you do even if your thoughts never reach paper will help you to improve your practice in the future and can inform the decisions you make about many issues – so try to do it from time to time.

Create a display showing children's work and encourage feedback from parents

Showing improvement

If you do get time, it's a great idea to take a notebook (or an academic diary) to record the steps you have taken to improve. For example, you might have faced an issue that many schools encounter when parents raise concerns about how often their children's reading books are changed. Under the heading *Changing reading books* you might then decide to keep track of how often and when children's reading books are changed. Committing this information to paper may reveal that you have an established system that you understand but may not have communicated fully to parents, or it may show that there are some inconsistencies in your approach. Whatever your initial findings, you might wish to consider why parents are concerned about the frequency of book changes, for example, might a child have been reading the same book for four nights in a week, which raises the issue of whether this a good use of time and a motivator for a beginning reader. With this information you might decide to trial a system which encourages children and their parents to independently choose books of the same reading level in-between the times that staff change their reading books. Recording the process by which you achieve a satisfactory outcome will inform your self-evaluation.

This may be particularly helpful if you are looking to move jobs or applying for promotion since interviewers often want to know about real examples of your work with children, so it is worth putting together a folder so that you can share some of those things when the opportunity arises. You might also add photographs to show developments – begin with a picture of where you started and add others to show how things changed over time. You might feel that an area of provision in your setting is under-used and that children don't access certain opportunities, such as reading for pleasure. A review of the use of your book area may show that children prefer to curl up with a book in a quiet spot away from the designated book area. By observing this area, you may decide it is missing the mark for a number of reasons. Taking some photographs of the book area and displaying these could be the start of a conversation with the children about its good and bad points. Displaying the photographs, together with sticky notes of children's responses will encourage children to contribute their opinions. Once these have been sought children will enjoy helping to make the area more user-friendly and monitoring usage will be part of the fun of finding out whether their ideas were successful. Recording this process in a floor book or in a display will show the stages that were gone through before the perfect book area was created with the help of everybody in the class.

Documenting your journey is the start of reflective practice and leads to a cycle of continuing improvement – which of course brings a fresh approach to teaching and learning.

Identifying your strengths and any areas for development

Accurate self-evaluation is the key to success for all organisations, big or small. Why? Because our desire to improve is more focused when we set our own priorities. This is because our self-esteem remains intact if we are able to identify our areas of improvement, rather than have them pointed out by an outsider, even an expert outsider. However, taking the time to reflect on our practice, rather than getting on with the job of doing it can sometimes leave us feeling like we are neglecting our priorities, in favour of doing things which will help us to get through each day. This chapter is intended to help you identify your strengths so that you can reflect on all the good things you are doing right now – these may relate to any number of things including your relationships with parents, children, colleagues and others. The following is a quick self-assessment guide; it is not intended to diagnose management issues, rather it is intended to act as a 'dip-stick', helping you take a look at your provision from the outside! Take a look at the following five areas (bold) and rate yourself in relation to each strand, using the headings in the columns to guide you:

Table 1.1 Identifying strengths and areas for development

Strength	Established	Developing	On my radar	Something I should consider
Excellent relationships with:				
Parents				
(and between) Children				
Colleagues				
Partners (such as feeder settings)				
Excellent deployment of other adults:				
Roles and responsibilities are set out in job descriptions				
Roles and responsibilities are communicated effectively to each team member				
Learning objectives for groups and individuals are shared and teaching input is accurate for every child				

Strength	Established	Developing	On my radar	Something I should consider
Key person responsibilities are clearly set out and team members act as a substitute for colleagues when necessary				
Every key person is given support in ways of working with parents				
All adults fully understand their roles in regard to teaching and learning				
Excellent organisation of the indoor space:				
Areas of provision are attractive and well-resourced				
Signage indicates maximum number of children in an area at any time				
Sign-in or self-registration system with hook and loop fasteners in place to encourage children to choose areas (rather than flit between them)				
Resources accessible and labelled with pictures and words				
Resources enhanced or changed in line with new areas of interest				
Resources regularly reviewed and checked so that they are in good condition, complete and in good working order, e.g. sharp pencils, cleaned whiteboards				
Consumable resources such as paper, paints, felt pens regularly reviewed, varied and replenished				
Books and props regularly checked for wear and tear				

Strength	Established	Developing	On my radar	Something I should consider
Books and props changed regularly to maintain children's attention and reflect current interests				
Cloakrooms and toilets well-maintained and well-lit				
Cloakroom area uncramped and pegs and boxes easily accessible				
Parents' board and literature accessibly placed and consistently updated, attractive and in parent-friendly language				
Displays backed in robust material so that backing lasts throughout the year				
Displays showing children's work (and processes leading to it) labelled				
Interactive displays that encourage children to a) use them, e.g. with removable signs or lift the flap information and b) to display their own choice of 'work'				
Displays changed regularly so that they don't become like 'wallpaper'				
Excellent organisation of the outdoor space:				
Area is attractive and inviting in all seasons				
Zones are clearly set out and resources are easily accessed				
Zones provide for a range of activities including vigorous movement, climbing, digging, quiet area, growing, sensory area				

Strength	Established	Developing	On my radar	Something I should consider
A range of equipment is available dependent on children's interests and the weather				
Open-ended resources support imaginative and creative activities and critical thinking				
Photos of each zone guide adults and children to ensure they leave areas ready for others after use				
Excellent opportunities for learning and development:				
Children are motivated, interested and eager to learn				
Assessment-led planning meets the needs of all children				
Children's interests are referred to and evident in most planning				
Children are engaged in a range of open-ended experiences for significant parts of the day				
Experiences and activities on offer effectively support children's learning in the prime areas of the EYFS				
Experiences and activities on offer effectively support children's learning in the specific areas of the EYFS				
Experiences and activities on offer effectively support children in developing the CoEL				
Play and learning opportunities are available both in and out of doors				

Once you have rated your environment for learning using the broad areas in Table 1.1, you can then analyse your strengths and any areas for development from the following:

Table 1.2 Analysis of strengths and areas for development

	Your score	Total (max)	Strengths	Areas to develop
Excellent relationships		12		
Excellent deployment of other adults		18		
Excellent organisation of the indoor space		48		
Excellent organisation of the outdoor space		18		
Excellent opportunities for learning and development		24		

You might now want to consider the reasons for your success in some areas. Are you particularly keen on outdoor learning (and as a consequence you have scored top marks in this area) or is it that you are a people person and have scored amazingly in relationships? You could, if you have time, invite a colleague to work with you on considering your strengths because modesty often deters many of us from owning what we do well, and instead pushes us towards magnifying our faults! Nevertheless, whatever your strengths are you should celebrate them since, as we all know, success breeds success and finding your strengths can be a great motivator, spurring you on to greater heights of professional development.

Having identified your strengths, you may wonder why other areas are less developed. The reasons may be simple or complex, for example, you may have had little experience of managing others and when it comes to the deployment of a Teaching Assistant (TA) you may feel intimidated because the person is older or more experienced than you are. Alternatively, you may have inherited an outdoor area which has not been planned or developed suitably for the children in your class and is therefore dull and falls short of the excellent standard you would like to provide. Ultimately, some issues may fall within your domain of influence, whilst others may be beyond your control. Therefore, there will be some things you can change right away, some that will take time and others that you cannot achieve without help.

An example of something you can change right away would be to ensure that all adults and children know how many children can use an area of provision, such as the home corner, at any one time. You can do this by consulting with adults and children about what would be a sensible number then displaying this in the appropriate area, reminding everybody of the limit. This is a quick win. For those things you can only change over time, such as children being independent in getting ready for PE, you need to be patient because this is an area which may take a considerable time, beginning with galvanising parental support and then helping different children to focus on small tasks, such as putting their clothes in a certain spot so they can find them again or taking off their shoes independently. Other things which you can't achieve on your own and are beyond your control you may have to live with and even make the most of, for example, you might have access from your classroom to a grassed area that becomes a mud flat in the rain – this isn't something that can be changed immediately, so in these circumstances you have to take the long-term approach. Decide what needs to be done and see if you can work magic by involving others such as parents and governors in helping to bring about the desired change. It may be though, that in the interim, you can make a reed garden or a mud splashing pit!

Peer review

Some schools benefit from involving EYFS colleagues from other schools to share effective practice and explore concerns together. I have facilitated this approach with schools that are organised into learning networks. This approach ensures that the issues explored are relevant and important to the people involved, closely related to each school's improvement plan and focused on providing continuing professional development for all involved, including the facilitator.

Key takeaway

After deliberating about your practice, seeking feedback from others and evaluating what you can do to bring about improvements, you may want to record this in some way so that you:

a) stay on track
b) focus on just a small number of priorities at once
c) prove to yourself what a difference you have made.

To do this, you may want to create a plan setting out your priorities for action in the area(s) you feel is/are of most concern to you right now. You should try to develop these plans over the following half term or so – any less time and you may not succeed; any more time and you may lose focus. Try to think of your plan as a travel itinerary, showing possible routes for future exploration but don't attempt to try to visit all the places at once! Having selected just one of the broad areas to start with, plan over time to address each of the remaining areas. The following simple format could be completed by setting targets for improvement. If you use it, try to make the steps you intend to take both realistic and manageable.

Table 1.3 Action plan

What needs to change?	What will be done? (actions to be taken)	When will this change be completed?	What difference will the change make?
1.			
2.			
3.			

Remember self-evaluation is about recognising and celebrating your own strengths and identifying practice issues which concern you. Your own self-evaluation can inform the school's self-evaluation but there is no requirement for this – the spur should be about your own professional development. Ironically, once we start this process it becomes a journey that never ends because when we reflect and act on our thoughts we inevitably find that we are making new discoveries about our own abilities and about our practice. Reflection leads to evaluation and evaluation leads to a fresh start or a new direction. New beginnings are wonderfully motivating and uplifting and, remember, since variety is the spice of life we often thrive on the changes we create. In the next chapters I will discuss ways we can continue to explore and reflect on what is done now and then consider what else could be done to make practice even better!

Sources

Ofsted school inspection handbook August 2018

- 'Ofsted **does not require self-evaluation to be provided in a specific format**. Any assessment that is provided should be part of the school's business processes and not generated solely for inspection purposes.' (Page 10)

- 'Leaders and managers have an accurate picture of the strengths and weaknesses of the provision **as a result of effective self-evaluation**. The impact of concerted and effective action to improve provision, including the training and development of staff, can be seen in children's achievement.' (Page 62)

Teachers' standards 2013

'**Appropriate self-evaluation, reflection and professional development activity is critical to improving teachers' practice** at all career stages.' (Page 4)

'TEACHING: A teacher must:

- **reflect systematically on the effectiveness of lessons** and approaches to teaching.' (Page 8)

NASUWT (2015) Guidance for Teachers

- '**It is important that self-evaluation is not burdensome** or bureaucratic. School leaders should ensure that their school self-evaluation practice draws together school improvement planning, performance management and audit, and that it supports effective teaching and learning. School self-evaluation should not be an additional process and it should not involve additional monitoring and evaluation, including classroom observation. It should not involve teachers undertaking additional responsibilities or require them to be subject to any additional processes or meetings.

- **Self-evaluation should support school improvement**. It should not create unnecessary workload and it should not start from the presumption that teachers must be monitored because they cannot be trusted.

- The record of any self-evaluation, including the summary report, should not include information about individual staff or information that allows staff to be identified.' (Page 26)

2 What to do when: Planning for learning

Key points

- Successful planning is about getting enough of the details right so that you meet the requirements of the EYFS at the same time as creating plans that work
- Planning approaches vary but if you focus on developing a range of experiences for your children you can then identify potential learning and possible lines of enquiry
- Distinguish broad planning intentions over the year by using different coloured highlighter pens for each medium or half term plan
- Remember plans are working documents, so ensure they are fit for purpose and don't be afraid to make notes on them to show differentiation and changes of direction

Successful planning

Whether you are teaching a nursery or Reception class, the curriculum is drawn from the seven areas of learning in the EYFS, together with how you plan to support children's play and learning so they make progress over time. If, like me, you have ever organised an event such as a party or a project, you know that the most important thing you have to do to ensure its success is to plan every detail. This approach generally holds good whenever we want something to go well. The same is true of planning for play and learning in your EYFS class or unit. Planning should be focused on what children can do now and the opportunities you are going to provide to enable them to develop further.

Whenever you start to think about planning, that is, what to do and when to do it, you will have to begin by considering your school, your learning environment and your children and staff. A good starting point for guiding your thinking is to focus on the question: What planning do I need?

Planning in the EYFS for three- to five-year-olds

There is no given quantity or format for planning in the EYFS, and what works for one school will not necessarily work for another. Each setting will also have various requirements. Within any planning document, schools must be able to show how they are considering the *'individual needs, interests and stage of development of each child'* and how they are using this to plan *'challenging and enjoyable experiences'* (DfE, 2017:9) for each child in all of the seven areas of learning and development. But, how much and what type of planning is down to individual choice and the needs of your children and your setting? Is there any specific time allocation for child-initiated or adult-led activities? This is an ongoing judgment made by practitioners; that decision comes down to your professional judgement. The EYFS does, though, state that practitioners should incorporate the following elements into their planning, visually:

- **Child-initiated** – where the adult sets up the learning environment to ensure children can be independent in their play, based on children's needs and interests. This may involve adults but springs from the child's ideas.
- **Adult-guided** – where the adult supports the child to develop their own learning.
- **Adult-led** – where the adult decides the activity, the learning intentions and goals and supports the children through the activity.

The important thing here is that you make all opportunities playful and that you get the balance right for the needs of your children.

Children creating their own number stories using resources the adult has introduced

Planning approaches

It's fairly obvious that we cannot extend children's learning until we know what they can do and what experiences they have had, so that we can build from there. Planning must therefore start with observation (see Chapter 3 if you want to consider this now) – this tells us what children enjoy and what they can do so that we can identify experiences, resources, interactions and activities to extend their learning and development. Consequently, one major advantage of planning is that it is the key way in which we can build on children's interests and meet their needs (see Chapter 6 for more on this). Planning may be presented in any number of ways, so you can choose how to present it, unless your school has its own format.

Children's interests

As a starting point, based on what you know about the children, you could begin by creating some skeleton planning every two to four weeks. This would allow you enough time to gather your resources such as books and other items that will excite and interest the children. At this stage, any planning will relate to the interests of the children, their particular needs and the predictable events you have planned for the weeks ahead, such as a book week or a theatre visit.

Who should be involved in planning?

- **Children** – planning should come from the children's interests and meet their individual learning needs. It is stressed in the EYFS, which is inclusive, that every child is unique so this should be evident in your planning.
- **Parents** – a big focus of the EYFS is on home learning and involving parents in their child's education.
- **Key workers** – using their knowledge of their key children (some gained from feeder settings or a previous class or school) and their observations of children's play to inform planning and identify next steps in learning.

Broad planning intentions

Plans can be developed a couple of times each half term, which, when put together at the end of a year, would constitute a long-term plan (for reflection purposes). This is the basic structure to all your other planning and equates to the stage in party planning when you are thinking how many guests will be invited and what type of refreshments and entertainment you will be providing for them. For existing examples of planning try school websites such as www.shadworthinfants.co.uk/reception-1/, or use Google to find websites of other schools you know.

Below is a record of the thinking behind a very simple plan for Summer 2 showing some of the things a school might plan to do based around children's needs, interests and the time of year. There is no requirement for it to be written down but if it is written down, it will remind team members of why certain experiences were provided. This is important because we can sometimes overlook why something was planned and focus more strongly on the outcomes rather than on the process of an activity. If you develop your plans at your staff meeting with colleagues you can then collectively evaluate these plans every week, exchanging and jotting down ideas about what worked and what was less successful.

Table 2.1 Simple plan for Summer 2

Predictable events this half term	Purpose (what we think children may gain from this)	Potential outcome (some of the possible lines of enquiry that may come from the experience)
Trip to Maple Farm	• First-hand experience of visiting a farm • Learn the names of different animals and the sounds they make, what they eat and where they live • Names of structures and buildings: byre, kennel, etc. • Opportunity to follow a map of Maple Farm and talk about routes round the farm (linking with: *What the Ladybird Heard* by Julia Donaldson and Lydia Monks and *Handa's Surprise* by Eileen Browne) • Could lead into story maps as well as topographical maps!	• Talking about different places and living things (UW) • New vocabulary related to farms to link with *What the Ladybird Heard* by Julia Donaldson and Lydia Monks and *Handa's Surprise* by Eileen Browne – two of our favourite authors • Making up rhymes (C&L and Literacy) • Recalling events • Exploring maps and planning journeys (C&L and UW/Maths) • Using story framework to re-invent their own stories
Chicken eggs to be hatched	• Children could observe, photograph and talk about the conditions for the eggs to hatch • We could read non-fiction books and stories that focus on the life cycle • Learning new vocabulary, e.g. shell, fragile, crack, open, hatch, small, tiny, weak, torch, candling, heat lamp	• Focusing on self-care and care for other living things (PD and UW) • Observing change (UW) • Counting and predicting how many eggs will hatch each day (Maths) Possible questions: • How does an incubator work? • Why do the eggs need to be kept warm?

	• Children may want to set up their own incubator in a tuff tray using materials such as straw, water and torches	• How long will it take for all the eggs to hatch? • How long will it take for one chick to hatch? • Why do you need to put water in? • What can we see when we shine the torch?
Forest School (Wed pm)	• Talk about which plants are safe to eat and why • Which plants we should not touch or eat • Every child can find out about foraging safely for herbs and grasses to make potions or other mixtures • Quieter children to be encouraged to be leaders as they collect blackberries and tip them from the small containers into the wooden tub	• Develop independence and self-confidence by taking risks • Trying out new things such as finding and gathering blackberries • Making potions, using a range of plants and herbs (PSED and PD)
Transition Story Times (Thurs am) Terms 2 and 3	• Children will have a chance to get to know their new teacher and TA so that by the time they move up they will be confident and familiar with the Y1 class • Become familiar with resources in the Y1 class so that they feel confident about moving 'up'	• Exploring growing independence • Adapting to new staff • Finding out about their new environment • Identifying their favourite place in the new classroom (PSED and C&L)
Mr Music Maker Workshop	• The children really enjoy making sounds and singing – many of them like watching 'The Voice', 'X Factor' and other programmes on TV • Finding out about ways to improvise sounds and make their own music • Learn the names of different instruments such as a mouth organ, guitar, cymbals • Explore voice and body sounds • Encourage boys to become involved as they don't seem to use the fixed sound-making equipment outside as much as the girls do	• Finding out about the different instruments Mr Music Maker plays • Exploring how the sounds he makes on improvised sound makers such as gutters, bottles and pipes can be changed • Developing ideas for making their own sound makers • Developing rhythms and moving to sounds (EAD and C&L) • Differentiating sounds, sound discrimination, cadence and voice control

| New Starters Visits, 1, 2 and 3 Term 3 | • Just as our children need to become familiar with the Y1 class, we recognise how helping the children who will be new to our class in September will give our children a big confidence boost. Each child will choose a child to 'buddy up' with
• They will share a coat peg and introduce them to things they enjoy doing
• Our children will help our visitors to choose a snack and a drink and show them our lovely outdoor area
• They will give the new children a picture of their key person | • Talking about and finding ways to help new children settle and enjoy their visit
• Thinking about what they like and what the new children would like
• Taking photograph of the areas for the new children so that they can show them where they can play and what they can do during the visit
• Making links with how it felt to be new in their Y1 class and how it will feel to be new in Reception (PSED) |

Planning should take account of events and visits such as a trip to the farm

Identifying outcomes

When you have developed your thinking and made a note of your ideas as shown in Table 2.1 you can then take a copy of the Early Years Outcomes and highlight any relevant statements in the areas of learning showing the focus of your thinking. These simply identify a direction for your planning so there is no need to adhere to them slavishly. If you use a different coloured highlighter each half term you will be able to review and evaluate how your plans are progressing and what learning is taking place. When these broad learning objectives are identified for the whole group, you can then extend or break them into smaller steps for individuals, or groups of children, which will give you a sharper focus for your teaching.

Characteristics of effective learning

At this point, another thing you should consider is 'how' children learn as opposed to 'what' they learn. This is referred to in the EYFS as the Characteristics of Effective learning (DfE/EE, 2012b: 6–7) shown in Table 2.2. Your planning should therefore identify opportunities for children to engage in these processes.

Once you have considered the Characteristics of Effective Learning (CoEL), it is then simple to add these on to a sheet which will become your medium- or short-term plan. In Table 2.2 reference is made to development band 40–60+ months and/or to the Early Learning Goals (ELGs), as well as relevant aspects of the CoEL. However, further notes (differentiation) could also be made in relation to particular groups and individuals to show that you are aware of the varying needs of your class. Differentiation could include making provision for a child who is awaiting an Education, Health and Care (EHC) plan who requires support at periods of change such as when a visit is being made; or for a group of children whose language development may need more support; as well as for a child with learning delay or a very able child who is developing more quickly than their peers. In order to meet the needs of these children additional notes could be added to extend the potential outcomes. To do this, it will be important to amend, extend or modify your plans to show that you are catering for any specific needs (handwriting is fine), remembering that: *'A pupil has SEN where learning difficulty or disability calls for special educational provision, namely provision different from or additional to that normally available to pupils of the same age'* (DFE/DOH, 2015:94).

The basic plan

You now have a basic plan. You may also want to extend this by adding what learning could potentially occur over the given period in any of the areas of provision, as well as any planned teaching that may not be covered in sufficient detail in the medium- or short-term plans, such as phonics sessions based on programmes like Letters and Sounds (appropriate to the ages/stages of children). In Table 2.3 you can see that alongside each of the EYFS areas of learning one or more of the CoEL has been added. This is just one way to show these – many teachers add several of the characteristics to their plans in a separate box.

Table 2.2 Characteristics of Effective Learning

Playing and Exploring (Engagement)	Active Learning (Motivation)	Creative and Thinking Critically (Thinking)
Finding out and exploring • Showing curiosity about objects, events and people • Using senses to explore the world around them • Engaging in open-ended activity • Showing particular interests	**Being involved and concentrating** • Maintaining focus on their activity for a period of time • Showing high levels of energy, fascination • Not easily distracted • Paying attention to details	**Having their own ideas** • Thinking of ideas • Finding ways to solve problems • Finding new ways to do things
Playing with what they know • Pretending objects are things from their experience • Representing their experiences in play • Taking on a role in their play • Acting out experiences with other people	**Keeping on trying** • Persisting with activity when challenges occur • Showing a belief that more effort or a different approach will pay off • Bouncing back after difficulties	**Making links** • Making links and noticing patterns in their experience • Making predictions • Testing their ideas • Developing ideas of grouping, sequences, cause and effect
Being willing to 'have a go' • Initiating activities • Seeking challenge • Showing a 'can do' attitude • Taking a risk, engaging in new experiences, and learning by trial and error	**Enjoying achieving what they set out to do** • Showing satisfaction in meeting their own goals • Being proud of how they accomplished something – not just the end result • Enjoying meeting challenges for their own sake rather than external rewards or praise	**Choosing ways to do things** • Planning, making decisions about how to approach a task, solve a problem and reach a goal • Checking how well their activities are going • Changing strategy as needed • Reviewing how well the approach worked

Early Education/Department for Education (2012), Development Matters

The most important thing is that you focus on these in your plans to the same degree as you do on the aspects and areas of learning.

So, that's the first step. You have thought about the children you will be teaching; you have identified any predictable or fixed events; you have identified any potential learning, including how children will have opportunities to develop the CoEL and now you are ready to consider how your plans will unfold! In other words, what you will do to make the party a success (obviously, when it comes to parties, you need the venue, the refreshments and entertainment and the guests). In school it's slightly different, though you still have the guests (children), the venue (your learning environment), and the 'refreshments and entertainment' (the experiences that will help the children to learn).

Table 2.3 Medium-term plan for Summer 2

AREA OF LEARNING and CoEL	AREA OF LEARNING and CoEL
PSED: Making relationships • Explains own knowledge and understanding, and asks appropriate questions of others **PSED: Managing feelings and behaviour** • Understands that our own actions affect other people • Aware of the boundaries set, and of behavioural expectations in the setting **PSED: Self-confidence and self-awareness** • Children are confident to try new activities and say why they like some activities more than others	**PHYSICAL: Moving and handling** • They move confidently in a range of ways, safely negotiating space **PHYSICAL: Health and self-care** • Shows understanding of the need for safety when tackling new challenges, and considers and manages some risks • Shows understanding of how to transport and store equipment safely • Practises some appropriate safety measures without direct supervision
CoEL: • Initiating activities • Seeking challenge • Showing a 'can do' attitude	**CoEL:** • Taking a risk, engaging in new experiences and learning by trial and error
MATHEMATICS: Numbers • Uses the language of 'more' and 'fewer' to compare two sets of objects • Finds the total number of items in two groups by counting all of them • Says the number that is one more than a given number • Finds one more or one less from a group of up to five objects, then ten objects • In practical activities and discussion, beginning to use the vocabulary involved in adding and subtracting • Records, using marks that they can interpret and explain	**LITERACY: Reading** • Enjoys an increasing range of books • Knows that information can be retrieved from books and computers **LITERACY: Writing** • Writes own name and other things such as labels, captions • Attempts to write short sentences in meaningful contexts
CoEL: • Developing ideas of grouping, sequences, cause and effect	**CoEL:** • Showing high levels of energy, fascination • Not easily distracted • Paying attention to details
EAD: Exploring and using media and materials • Explores the different sounds of instruments **EAD: Being Imaginative** • They represent their own ideas, thoughts and feelings, music and dance (ELG)	**KNOWLEDGE AND UNDERSTANDING: The World** • Looks closely at similarities, differences, patterns and change
CoEL: • Representing their experiences in play • Making links and noticing patterns in their experience • Testing their ideas	**CoEL:** • Showing curiosity about objects, events and people • Making predictions

AREA OF LEARNING and CoEL
COMMUNICATION AND LANGUAGE
Understanding • Children follow instructions involving several ideas or actions • They answer 'how' and 'why' questions about their experiences and in response to stories or events **Speaking** • Uses talk to organise, sequence and clarify thinking, ideas, feelings and events • Uses language to imagine and recreate roles and experiences in play situations
CoEL: • Representing their experiences in play

When the unexpected happens

To ensure you organise these things effectively, you may decide that you will create continuous provision plans for different areas and weekly plans that will focus you in terms of particular aspects of learning (and the roles of team members at key points in the day) or you may choose to create daily plans. The choice is yours. Very often, less is more in planning because your plans should be flexible to ensure that unpredictable events can be accommodated. However, whatever you decide, you should always be able to say 'That's under control' to each of the following questions:

If you were unexpectedly absent:

- How would a supply teacher know what was planned?
- How would each team member know what they were going to be doing during each session?
- How would team members ensure that children didn't lose out on learning opportunities?

If to all three questions you can say: 'I have a plan for that' – then fine, no worries. If you can't answer all three questions in the affirmative then consider drawing up some simple plans that address each issue. Then place them where they can be seen. As a minimum provide:

a) a rota showing which zones of the indoor and outdoor environments will be managed by which members of staff at which times

b) details of any fixed events such as PE or Forest School sessions

c) an outline of the focus of learning for the week in relation to the EYFS areas of learning.

How and what you plan is largely up to you. Too much planning can become unwieldy and unhelpful and over-planning may inhibit spontaneity and make for a dull menu, so only plan for short periods because things may not go the way you imagined. Therefore, it's also important when planning to get all the help you can, from other people, so that your planning accurately reflects the current interests of the children in your class.

Planned inputs

No discussion of planning would be complete without consideration of what should be recorded about all the teaching tasks which most EYFS teachers feel they have to 'fit in', such as guided reading and writing, hearing individual readers, literacy or maths inputs or one-off sessions such as those provided to cover teachers' preparation and planning (PPA) time, for example, music, PE or a foreign language.

You may wish to draft a timetable setting out when planned inputs such as guided reading will take place, identifying who will do what. Learning intentions will be drawn from the medium-term plans in the different areas of learning and whether you choose to work with the whole class or groups of children is up to you. BUT remember the activities and experiences should be challenging and enjoyable and should range between those purely decided on by the adults (adult-led) to those that spring directly or indirectly from the child (child-initiated and adult-guided). Indeed, consulting and involving children about planning is important since this approach will ensure that they, like you, are invested in the learning process.

Again, how you develop planning for such activities is a professional judgement and you are the best judge of what is necessary. However, if you want to get the best from the time adults (other than you) are teaching it is probably wise to identify what you want from them and then take time to share this with them. If you are lucky enough to have the services of a music teacher it would be important to tell them about your plans for 'Mr Music Maker' so that they don't ruin your workshop plans by introducing the children to the instruments they will be finding out about at that event! Similarly, if somebody takes your class for PE or dance then ensure that you direct the children's learning by identifying what you want that adult to provide for them. If, on the other hand, children are learning a foreign language ensure that you know what they are doing in each session so that links can be made in-between times and their learning won't be lost, because children have learned to count in French or Spanish during these sessions but rarely get chance to share what they know. Remember if something is worth doing it's worth doing well!

Is your planning fit for purpose?

The questions and the responses in Table 2.4 may help you evaluate your current planning.

Key takeaway

Your planning is fit for purpose if…
a) It references the EYFS areas of learning and CoEL
b) Is based on observation of children and reflects their interests, needs and ways of learning

c) It clearly informs adults who work with you of their roles and responsibilities in teaching and learning

d) It is equally rigorous in regard to outdoor and indoor opportunities

e) It is used as a working document (which you annotate as necessary) because it relates to this particular cohort of children in this particular class at this particular time: that is, it is a real reflection of the learning journeys that the children in your class are taking at the current time.

Evaluation of practice: planning

Check out the different types of planning in Table 2.5 and assess whether you need it or want it. When you have decided, complete the column stating the rationale behind your decision for choosing the types of planning you use currently.

Table 2.4 Fit for purpose: planning?

QUESTION	NEGOTIABLE OR NON-NEGOTIABLE?	YOUR RESPONSE
Are children's individual needs and interests reflected?	*Non-negotiable: This is a requirement of the EYFS.*	
Can you show how observations link to planning?	At the start of a year or if you have new children in your group it may not always be possible to do this from the outset, so you should consider what is age/stage appropriate given what you know about your cohort. To do this you should try to access any information about the children from them, their family and the previous setting/class. *Non-negotiable: Once children attend your setting your observations should inform planning.*	
Do your plans relate to all seven areas of learning and development?	*Non-negotiable: This is a requirement of the EYFS. However, there should be a strong emphasis on the prime areas for younger children to support their development in the specific areas.*	
Are you showing how your provision and activities support children to make progress?	That is, have you identified children's starting points and have you planned around their interests and next steps for learning? And, are you keeping track of this through staff meetings to review the progress of individuals and groups of children?	
Does your planning cover outdoor experiences as well as those which take place indoors?	The best approach to thinking about this is that just as the indoor area is intended as an environment for learning so is the outdoor environment. However, the play that occurs in the outdoor area may well be different because of what you provide and what children can choose to do. *Non-negotiable: It is a requirement of the EYFS that you 'must provide access to an outdoor play area or, if that is not possible, ensure that outdoor activities are planned and taken on a daily basis' (DfE, 2017:30).*	
Does your planning show how you will support children to develop the Characteristics of Effective Learning?	*Non-negotiable. This is the 'how' of play and learning – and describes children's attitudes such as their motivation, their inventiveness or their determination to succeed.*	

Table 2.5 Rationale for planning

Type of Plan	My thoughts	The rationale behind my decision is:
Short- or Medium-term Plans	These can help us to get an overview of the weeks ahead such as a half term. They can help us maintain focus on broad learning intentions at any particular time.	
Weekly Plans	These contain the details of what you hope to achieve over a week (drawn from a medium-term plan) but they should be flexible and easily changed in line with children's interests.	
Daily Plans	This may show more detail such as resources and the names of the children changing their reading books or acting out a story with a student's help.	
Continuous Provision Plans	When you set up an area, you are planning to a certain extent what will take place in that area. Any decision about what areas you provide in your class is entirely up to you but if you want children to learn when they are in these areas you do need to carefully plan what stimuli will be provided to support well-developed play and learning.	
Adult Roles Plans	This might be a simple plan showing days, times and responsibilities of any adults, including students.	
Lesson Plans: Literacy, Phonics, Maths, RE, Circle time, Story time, etc.	If discrete sessions are planned the main focus of these could indicate the specifics of the session. You might also want to add timings, expectations and success criteria drawn from the short- or medium-term plans for the relevant areas of learning.	

Sources

Ofsted school inspection handbook August 2018

- **'Ofsted does not require schools to provide individual lesson plans to inspectors.** Equally, Ofsted **does not** require schools to provide previous lesson plans.

- **Ofsted does not specify how planning should be set out, the length of time it should take or the amount of detail it should contain.** Inspectors are interested in the effectiveness of planning rather than the form it takes.' (Page 9)

- **'Provision across all areas of learning is planned meticulously.** It is based on rigorous and sharply focused assessments of children's achievement so that every child undertakes highly challenging activities.' (Page 65)

Statutory framework for the early years foundation stage: Setting the standards for learning, development and care for children from birth to five (2017)

The EYFS states:

'Each area of learning and development must be implemented through **planned, purposeful play and through a mix of adult-led and child-initiated activity.** Play is essential for children's development, building their confidence as they learn to explore, to think about problems, and relate to others. **Children learn by leading their own play, and by taking part in play which is guided by adults.** There is an **ongoing judgement to be made by practitioners about the balance between activities led by children, and activities led or guided by adults.** Practitioners must respond to each child's emerging needs and interests, guiding their development through warm, positive interaction. As children grow older, and as their development allows, it is expected that **the balance will gradually shift towards more activities led by adults,** to help children prepare for more formal learning, ready for Year 1.' (Page 9)

Teachers' standards 2013

'TEACHING: A teacher must:

- Set high expectations which inspire, motivate and challenge pupils
- Impart knowledge and develop understanding through effective use of lesson time
- Promote a love of learning and children's intellectual curiosity
- **Reflect systematically on the effectiveness of lessons and approaches to teaching**

- Contribute to the design and provision of an engaging curriculum within the relevant subject area(s).' (Page 7)

NASUWT (2015) Guidance for teachers

- 'The School inspection handbook... makes it clear that Ofsted does not require schools to provide inspectors with detailed lesson plans, or specify how planning should be set out.' (Page 25)

DFE/DOH (2015) Special educational needs and disability code of practice: 0 to 25 years: Statutory guidance for organisations which work with and support children and young people who have special educational needs or disabilities

- '6.5 A pupil has SEN where their learning difficulty or disability calls for special educational provision, namely provision different from or additional to that normally available to pupils of the same age. Making higher quality teaching normally available to the whole class is likely to mean that fewer pupils will require such support. Such improvements in whole-class provision tend to be more cost effective and sustainable.' (Page 94)

3 Where to start: Observation

Key points

- Less is more, so observation should focus on important aspects of children's learning (rather than on anything and everything a child does or says)
- Plan to observe different groups of children and/or individuals, on different days
- Link observations to the early years outcomes so that you have a clear picture of the areas of learning that you manage successfully as well as those that are under-represented
- If observations don't inform planning, or provide the information you require, they may be a waste of time

Less is more

Observation is an area where, with the latest software, a great deal of information is being gathered and sometimes teachers are concerned that although they have virtual space filled with observations these don't always inform planning. Before the advent of interactive software, observations were jotted down on sticky notes or scraps of paper whereas now, in many schools, tablets are ubiquitous and appear, in some cases, to be in use at all times. And, whilst gathering the information can be done at speed, harvesting it can sometimes be time-consuming and confusing because of the sheer number of items recorded.

However, in some schools there is a focus on ensuring that any observations retained in the system are of high quality. This is achieved by the early years leader acting as editor, reviewing all the observations daily, before they are finalised and entered into the electronic system. Clearly, this method may mean that some observations aren't used because they repeat the same information, such as when a child who is very interested in *PJ Masks* constantly returns to the same theme in their play by adopting Cat Boy's powers. Until the play moves forward there is little point in noting down what was said or done each time because it is unlikely to represent anything significant or new. However, when something new does happen, such as when a child, who previously never chose to explore sound, suddenly decides to be a pop singer, beating out a rhythm on a drum and moving in time to the music whilst singing the refrain to a well-known pop song, then this is something noteworthy and should be noted since this may act as a signpost towards their interests and strengths. Observing this event may provide practitioners with opportunities to consider the next steps for a child's learning in Expressive Arts and Design (EAD), taking into account the relevant part of the ELG for this aspect, visually: *'sing songs, make music and dance, and experiment with ways of changing them'* (DfE, 2017:12).

Seeing a child exploring sound for the first time may be noteworthy

The amount of information gathered is down to personal choice, that is, based on what adults consider to be relevant. Too little detail and there is not enough evidence; too much information and there is a risk of it not being manageable as well as the worry that it may be obscuring important information about the child, the provision, the curriculum and our teaching. How important is the process of observation and how much observation should we do? The EYFS refers to observation in relation to assessment indicating that assessment *'involves practitioners observing children to understand their level of achievement, interests and learning styles, and to then shape learning experiences for each child reflecting those observations'* (DfE, 2017:13). Since the assessment arrangements are part of the statutory EYFS document, this tells us that, in the EYFS, observation is a requirement, not a choice. Taken together with Ofsted's statement regarding the quality of early years provision, visually: *'Assessment is accurate and based on high quality observations'* (Ofsted, 2016:61), the significance regarding this requirement is unequivocal.

In deciding how much to observe and how to record observations and evidence of learning it is important to consider that teaching should not be compromised in favour of evidence-gathering. Indeed, it states in the Early Years Profile Handbook (EYFSP) that *'There is no requirement that evidence should be formally recorded or documented. Practitioners should keep paperwork to the minimum needed to illustrate, support and recall their knowledge of the child's attainment'* (STA, 2018:16). Consider the following questions (and my answers in italics underneath each one) that adults often ask about observations when they are in doubt about the amount and necessity of observations:

1. How many observations should we do each week?
   There is no set requirement – this is a choice.
2. How many should we do for each child?
   There is no set requirement – this is a choice.
3. What can we do if we don't manage to photograph a child doing something that was really significant?
   Evidence can be varied and at the end of the EYFS it is important to note that the Profile Handbook states: 'Evidence means any material, knowledge of the child, anecdotal incident or result of observation, or information from additional sources that supports the overall picture of a child's development' (STA, 2018:16).
4. Is it OK to write up an observation after the event or does it have to be done in 'real time'?
   Observations can be written retrospectively; it is far better to engage with the child (in terms of teaching) than slavishly reporting on their learning. This can be done later.
5. If several children are doing something together can the same observation be used?
   Yes, provided it is useful and informative.
6. Can one observation cover more than one area of learning?
   Yes, many observations reveal the child is learning in a variety of areas. For example, when a child engages in imaginary play in the home corner they may also be weighing, measuring or mark making and therefore demonstrating a range of skills and abilities.
7. We have loads of observations stored electronically but find it difficult to use them to inform our planning, should we print them all off?
   No! Just review what you have and see if you are getting rich observations that illustrate significant learning or whether you have too much repetitive material which is clogging the system.
8. Will Ofsted want to see records of children's achievement and our written observations?
   Ofsted will want to ensure that the quality of teaching is good; that is, that planning is informed by observations. How they do this is up to them but it is unlikely they will have the time or need to see either of the items identified.

9. We currently discuss our observations at the end of each day so that we can direct our teaching accordingly – should we minute our discussions?

Considering what children are working on at the end of each day sounds excellent but surely the notes made on your plans are sufficient without recording your discussions as well?

10. Our school has a policy that there should be an observation on every child at least once a week, is this right?

There are no right or wrong answers to this – but obviously your school policy dictates what you are required to do. However, if this is reviewed it is worth considering whether all the observations over a week are necessary since the EYFS profile states: 'In developing their policies, settings should consider how to minimise practitioner workload so that practitioners can focus their efforts on teaching' (STA, 2018:16). And, whilst this does refer to the end of the EYFS, this approach seems sensible for all age groups.

Observing different children on different days

As is obvious from the previous discussion, it makes sense, if at all possible, to ensure that the time spent in observing children's learning and development is worthwhile. This means that there is a balance to be struck between the time available for teaching and observation, so that, instead of having lots of insignificant observations, the school gathers fewer yet better quality observations that offer insights into a child's thinking and current agenda.

This doesn't mean that spontaneous observations – revealing nuggets of information – shouldn't be valued. But, rather than trying to observe all of the children for all of the time (beyond keeping a weather eye on their involvement), it may be much more effective to focus more systematically on individuals or groups of children, who are the focus for part, or all of a day. In this way a clearer picture will emerge of each child because none will be left 'unseen', as sometimes happens when more visible children who practitioners may find more rewarding (in terms of what can be gleaned about their play and learning) appear more frequently in observations.

Take for example, a scenario of a quiet girl (A), who is busying herself making a card for her brother's birthday and another girl (B), who is making a home for a cat – both are absorbed in their activity and neither is speaking. However, because there are more possibilities for what can be done by child B the practitioner quickly directs their attention towards her, suggesting that she could perhaps decorate the walls of the cat house with pictures of the cat's family. In moments, child B and the practitioner are deep in conversation about ways in which the cat's home could be developed so that it has a doorway and windows, meanwhile child A is left to her own devices. If this happens to the same children twice then it may be that a fuller picture of child B begins to develop than of child A, unless measures are taken to ensure that each child is the focus of at least one adult, on a regular basis, over a two- to three-week period. The way this is done will be through genuine interactions with children through which *'practitioners… respond to their own day-to-day observations about children's progress and observations…'* (DfE, 2017:13). The usefulness of an observation created in this manner is likely to be greater than one where, tablet in hand, the practitioner takes pictures of a child (or children) then spends time adding notes electronically.

That is not to say that this way of recording is not useful, or that it has no part to play in observation. It clearly does, and is used extensively, probably by the majority of schools. However, it is important to remember that by engaging with children, the practitioner is able to explore through dialogue the child's current thinking, ideas, skills and knowledge, something that may be less likely if they are just standing back and observing, whilst focusing their attention on capturing pictures. The simplest solution is to ensure that two or three children from each key group are the focus of observation during a week, whilst at the same time allowing time to include spontaneous observations when interesting learning stories emerge.

Developing a clear picture

Observations can be useful not only to understand what children know, say and can do, but also to throw light on your provision as well as your own strengths or interests – in other words – what is observed will reflect what is on offer in your EYFS provision. Having a clear picture of learning in your EYFS begins with analysing and identifying what your observations are telling you about children as learners. To do this you will no doubt reflect on the CoEL and on the developmental steps in each EYFS aspect and area of learning. From this you will instantly get an insight into the 'strong' areas and the 'gaps', i.e. the areas that are under-represented in observations of your class. This may also enlighten you about how you provide for the interests of different groups, such as boys and girls, or older and younger children in the same class. Complete Table 3.1 for each child in one of your class groups – you may want to identify three girls and three boys of high, low and medium ability – to focus you in thinking about the number of observations you have on each child for each aspect and to explore any reasons for differences between groups of children.

Table 3.1 Review of types of observations by area of learning and gender

NAME:		
Aspect of learning	**Number of observations**	**Exploration of why this is the case**
Communication and Language (C&L)		
Listening and attention		
Understanding		
Speaking		
Physical Development (PD)		
Moving and handling		
Health and self-care		
Personal, Social and Emotional Development (PSED)		
Self-confidence and self-awareness		
Managing feelings and behaviour		
Making relationships		

Aspect of learning	Number of observations	Exploration of why this is the case
Literacy		
Reading		
Writing		
Mathematics		
Numbers		
Shape, space and measures		
Understanding the World (UW)		
People and communities		
The world		
Technology		
Expressive Arts and Design (EAD)		
Exploring and using media and materials		
Being imaginative		

When you have completed your review of observations for the selected group you may find some surprises, but equally you may decide that you know the reasons for your findings. If you wish to explore these differences further complete Table 3.2 found on the companion website for the same group of children (showing the number of observations for each child in each aspect of learning) to discover where you need to be focusing your attention so that outcomes improve.

If, having completed this analysis, you find that there is a gap in terms of gender or areas of learning, reflect on the unspoken messages children are receiving about what is (and is not) important. This may mean that you need to both rethink the way you communicate with parents about their children's learning and/or you may need to review your provision to identify why certain areas or groups are under-represented. One of the strongest outcomes nationally in the EYFS is physical development, whilst the weakest outcomes are in reading and writing – how do your outcomes compare with these? If they are as good as or better than the national average you are doing well, but if they are not it may mean there is something you are not currently seeing or fully providing for.

One sure way of improving outcomes for children is through offering a wide range of learning opportunities and working with the staff team to make certain that everybody is aware of the potential learning in any activities or experiences children engage in. For example, many schools feel that boys underperform in writing in the EYFS – and because this is a national issue they may be reassured this relates to reasons such as physical immaturity, many boys choosing not to write and so on. However, some schools seem able to overcome such barriers and buck the trend in this area, whilst others do not achieve the same results. The issues in the example below had not been identified fully by the school in question until, through a process of peer review, the staff were able to stand back and look objectively at what was happening on 'Writing Day' in their Reception classes, where boys did not choose to write as often as girls.

CASE STUDY: WRITING DAY

Visualise two adjoining Reception classrooms, both hives of activity – adults and children intent on writing – because this is 'Writing Day'. Indoors, all the children are eagerly writing about dinosaurs, dragons and any number of things, yet outside in the adjacent play area only one child has gone into the huge writing area. He is not so much interested in writing, as in discovering what will happen to the marks he is making with a UV pen, when he crawls into a dark den to reveal the hidden marks.

Scanning the areas nearby it is plain to see there are many potential opportunities for children to write out of doors – but with few or no 'hooks' to draw children in these are not being taken up. Looking at the 'theatre' area, where space has been set aside to accommodate a stage, together with seats for an audience, not one mark-making tool is in evidence and nobody has considered inviting children to make a poster to advertise their 'show', or to create tickets for the performance or to number the seats and so on. Similarly a story area has been set out with books and props such as painted stones representing different story book characters, including a witch, however, no mark-making materials are in evidence. What has been provided to encourage writing are several large pieces of paper fixed to fences near to a water tray and other resources, yet although this is a writing day there isn't much use being made of these despite there being a willing adult positioned beside the water tray, valiantly attempting to encourage children to talk about what they are doing so that she can scribe their words.

So, why, in spite of the best efforts of adults at this school, were children (especially boys) not turning to writing in their play? It could have been that by the time they were able to go outside they had had enough of writing – an intense and demanding activity that required a great deal of focus and concentration, particularly since in the first half of the school year, the majority would be four-year-olds. It could have been that by the time these children were free to venture outside, after being engaged in writing indoors, that they needed time to 'chill out' or simply to be. It could also be that they thought 'real writing' went on indoors, where adults were championing their efforts and encouraging them to complete their writing.

In several schools I have worked with it does seem that the main reason for boys not writing is the tacit messages that are conveyed to them about the type of writing that is valued by the school (and therefore promoted). Plus, some children appear to see no reason to write and sometimes teachers indicate that some boys don't show any particular desire to write. If this is an issue in your school perhaps it is time to reflect on ways you can create or extend 'hooks' or 'invitations' that will draw boys in so that they want to write. Think about which of the following in Table 3.3 is likely to motivate boys to want to make marks, draw and write and then reflect on your own provision for these.

Table 3.3 Engaging boys in mark making

Provision for mark making, drawing and writing	Will it motivate boys to write?	Reflection on your provision for boys' writing
Café corner – notepad, pencils, diary, sticky notes, whiteboard, markers, calendar, telephone, blackboard, chalks		
Construction area – builder's caddy containing a range of writing tools, clipboard, tape measure, long ruler, squared paper, part rolls of wallpaper		

Provision for mark making, drawing and writing	Will it motivate boys to write?	Reflection on your provision for boys' writing
Book area (scary stories) – suggestion box for favourite stories, felt pens, black paper, white paper, chalks, ballpoint pens, torches, skull and cross bone hats		
Role play (camping) – maps, magnifying glasses, twig pens, mud and sticks, prospectors' flags to pinpoint treasure, instructions on how to catch and cook a fish, water, leaves, cooking pots		
Tuff tray – shaving foam with red gel food colouring streaked through it, sticks, combs, squishy snakes		
Role play (Pets Are Us) – three different sizes of a variety of soft toys, three sizes of boxes (for beds), three sizes of feeding bowls and other sundries, neon signs, felt pens, scales		
Role play (space station) – floating pens, silver paper to make rubbings (use over coins), IW or tablet, walkie-talkies, highlighter pens		
Small world (story retell) – story books, story cards from book, e.g. *What the Ladybird Heard* by Julia Donaldson and Lydia Monks, props such as maps, striped T-shirts, animals from story, tablet or recorder to record a story		
Shadow puppets – different characters such as Jack, the giant, the hen and Jack's mother from *Jack and the Beanstalk*, screen, card, pencils, scissors, sticks, speech bubbles (large enough to write on), story map, key words		
Outdoor role play (explorer's kit) – binoculars, nets, luggage labels, clipboards, bug bottles/specimen jars		

Useful observations

Without any doubt, it is really important to offer provision that appeals to different children and, in order to do this well, it is vital that we observe children to discover their interests so that through our provision we can inspire them to have a go at the things that don't come so easily to them, such as when a shy child is enthused enough to forget their shyness and join in with a dance or when a boisterous child is inspired to sit quietly alongside their friend with a book. It is important in such circumstances to know what triggered the child's decision or responses so that this strategy can be used again in different circumstances. Sometimes, a child may be willing to help another child out by doing something they wouldn't normally choose to do; this may explain why the boisterous child was choosing to sit with a friend. Consulting with parents about their children's interests is also helpful, since parents understand their children best and their knowledge of their child should be reflected in the curriculum you provide.

Key takeaway

Useful observations then, are those that help us to understand the child, their strengths and interests and their learning needs or next steps – if the information from observations doesn't help us to shape our planning its value is questionable.

Look at the following observations and decide which are useful in focusing adults on children's learning:

Azaan

Age: 4 years 6 months
Date: 17th May 2018

Azaan held the paintbrush in a whole hand grip and pressed down the blue paint saying, 'It's raining'. TA pointed to the marks he was making and said, 'They also look like spiders to me, Azaan'. Azaan grinned and nodded.

- **EAD** (Exploring materials): experiments to create different textures (40–60 months)
- **CoEL** (Active learning): being involved and concentrating; maintaining focus on their activity for a period of time

Cody

Age: 5 years 0 months

Date: 10th May 2018

Cody chose to mark make with the chalk which she held in a fist grip as she made zigzag lines along the path. TA asked what she was drawing – she said, 'It's a giant'.

- **Literacy** (Writing): gives meaning to marks they make as they draw, write and paint (40–60 months)
- **CoEL** (Active learning): enjoying achieving what they set out to do; showing satisfaction in meeting their own goals

Marcus

Age: 4 years 1 month

Date: 3rd May 2018

Marcus was poking a stick into a pile of damp leaves. He said, 'They keep coming out'. TA asked why he needed the stick. Marcus said, 'They'll come on it and I'll take them to a stone. They live under stones'.

- **UW** (The world): shows care and concern for living things and the environment (30–50 months)
- **CoEL** (Creating and thinking critically): making links and noticing patterns in their experience; (Active learning): showing high levels of energy, fascination

Zoha

Age: 4 years 3 months

Date: 27th March 2018

It was milk time and Zoha was putting the cartons on the table. Zoha said, 'I can count them: 1, 2, 3, 4, 5, 6, 7, 8, 9, 10!' pointing to each one. TA: 'What about these?' (more cartons of milk). Zoha: 'Ohh, I'll have to start again – I can't do it now.' TA: 'Where did you get up to?' Zoha: 'Ten'. TA: 'Well what's the next number after ten?' Zoha thought for a minute and said, '11'.

- **Mathematics** (Numbers): counts objects to ten and beyond, and beginning to count beyond ten; says the number that is one more than a given number (40–60+ months)

- **CoEL** (Active learning): paying attention to details; persisting with activity when challenges occur

Edie

Age: 3 years 1 month
Date: 12th March 2018

Edie played with the small world fairies. She kept waving her hand round and saying, 'It's flying'. At tidy-up time she put them away in the box.

- **Communication and Language** (Speaking): uses gestures, sometimes with limited talk (22–36 months)
- **CoEL** (Active learning): maintaining focus on their activity for a period of time

Jensen

Age: 3 years 3 months
Date: 28th February 2018

Jensen was pulling out all the boxes and tipping them into a pram in the home corner. TA: 'Where are you off to with all that stuff?' Jensen carried on without speaking until he had emptied every box. He said, 'Going to… shops'. TA: 'Remember to put them away when you come back'. Jensen smiled.

- **Communication and Language** (Speaking): beginning to use word endings (22–36 months)
- **CoEL** (Active learning): maintaining focus on their activity for a period of time

Lily

Age: 5 years 4 months
Date: 19th February 2018

Lily was holding a pencil between her thumb and fingers in a tripod grip. She wrote: 'I can jump' sounding out each letter of the words 'can' and 'jump' correctly. Then she wrote 'I can pl' forming each letter correctly – she wasn't sure how to write it so she went to the working wall and found the word 'play' and brought it back. She pointed to the letters of the word 'play' until she reached the 'a', then she wrote it. She pointed to the 'y' and wrote it. She struggled to form the 'y' correctly. TA said, 'When *a* and *y* sit together they say *ay* like in *play*'. Lily said, 'And *hay* and *day*' and then she grinned.

- **Literacy** (Reading): can segment the sounds in simple words and blend them; (Writing): uses a pencil and holds it effectively to form recognisable letters, most of which are correctly formed (40–60+ months)
- **CoEL** (Active learning): persisting with activity when challenges occur; (Creativity and thinking critically): planning, making decisions about how to approach a task, solve a problem and reach a goal

Noah

Age: 3 years 7 months
Date: 7th February 2018

Noah was very excited to see the new animal jigsaws and ran over to them when he came into nursery. He completed a ten-piece jigsaw independently and TA said, 'Well done, Noah'. Noah looked happy!

- **PSED** (Self-confidence and self-awareness): welcomes and values praise for what they have done (30–50 months)
- **CoEL** (Playing and exploring): initiating activities

Aiza

Age: 5 years 2 months
Date: 31st January 2018

When Sadie was upset because Jude took the bike from her, Aiza said, 'I'm your friend'. She walked over to Jude and said, 'It's Sadie's turn'. Jude said, 'OK' and gave the bike to Sadie.

- **PSED** (Making relationships): takes steps to resolve conflicts with other children, e.g. finding a compromise (40–60+ months)
- **CoEL** (Creating and thinking critically): finding ways to solve problems

Finn

Age: 4 years 5 months

Date: 24th January 2018

Finn asked for the goal posts to be set up. He lined up three footballs. Olivia, Cory and Max came to watch. He ran towards the first ball, aiming his foot to hit it. The ball didn't go into the net so Finn said, 'The next will' and again he ran towards the ball and aimed a kick at it. He missed again, but said, 'The next one will be a goal'. Finn kicked the third ball very firmly and it went straight into the net.

- **Physical Development** (Moving and handling): shows increasing control over an object in pushing, patting, throwing, catching or kicking it (40–60+ months)
- **CoEL** (Active learning): enjoying meeting challenges for their own sake rather than external rewards or praise

After reading through the observations try to identify why some are more useful than others by completing the table below:

Table 3.4 Useful observations

Observation	Useful – why?	Not useful – why?
Azaan (4 years 6 months)		
Cody (5 years 0 months)		
Marcus (3 years 1 month)		
Zoha (4 years 3 months)		
Edie (Age 3 years 1 month)		
Jensen (3 years 3 months)		
Lily (5 years 4 months)		
Noah (3 years 7 months)		

Observation	Useful – why?	Not useful – why?
Aiza (5 years 2 months)		
Finn (4 years 5 months)		

You may have found that some observations offer a real insight into children's development, their language, mathematical or thinking skills, whilst others may tell you about children's learning dispositions or characteristics. Others may lack sufficient detail to be useful. It may be helpful to share these examples with your team to explore why some are more useful than others and then to encourage staff to reflect on the value of observations which focus on key aspects of children's learning.

Sources

Ofsted school inspection handbook August 2018

'Grade descriptors for the effectiveness of the early years provision
Outstanding (1)

Assessment is accurate and based on **high quality observations**. It includes all those involved in the child's learning and development. Provision across all areas of learning is planned meticulously. It is based on rigorous and sharply focused assessments of children's achievement so that every child undertakes highly challenging activities.' (Page 61)

STA (2018) Early years foundation stage profile handbook

'Reliable and accurate assessment at the end of the EYFS is underpinned by the following principles:

- assessment is based primarily on the practitioner's knowledge of the child – **knowledge is gained predominantly from observation** and interaction in a range of daily activities and events.' (Page 11)

'Practitioners must make their final EYFS profile assessments based on all their evidence. "Evidence" means any material, knowledge of the child, anecdotal incident or result of observation, or information from additional sources that supports the overall picture of a child's development.

Evidence should come from day-to-day activity in the classroom and can be drawn from a variety of sources. The type of evidence will vary from setting to setting, class to class, and even child to child. The form of evidence supporting a practitioner judgement is entirely up to the practitioner. Practitioners should avoid excessive evidence gathering.

There is no requirement that evidence should be formally recorded or documented. Practitioners should keep paperwork to the minimum needed to illustrate, support and recall their knowledge of the child's attainment.

A setting's assessment policy should outline when it is necessary to record evidence. In developing their policies, settings should consider how to minimise practitioner workload so that practitioners can focus their efforts on teaching.' (Page 16)

4 What next: Assessment

Key points

- Involve parents in identifying what their children can do and what their next steps should be
- On-entry assessment helps to orient you on the unique map of each child's development, at the start of their learning journey
- Ongoing assessment keeps you abreast of children's progress and helps you to support their learning over time
- Summative assessment allows you to reflect on what you know about each child at the end of their time with you so that you can share this with their parents and their next teacher/school

This chapter is based on the belief that when we assess less and teach more, children learn better. Assessment in the early years is a contentious area, particularly since the English government's announcement of its intention to introduce 'tests' for four-year-olds on entry to the Reception year. This raises some interesting issues about the nature of different types of assessment in school and what, if anything, such a measure can tell teachers about children's individual starting points so that they can provide learning opportunities that are appropriate for the age and stage of each child. However, in and of itself, assessment can be a useful strategy, provided its purpose is to inform teachers about children's strengths, interests and learning needs. If it is not used in this way it becomes a test which is, of course, unhelpful since learning in the EYFS was never designed around a measurable body of knowledge. This does not mean that assessment is not appropriate in the EYFS, since it is mandatory firstly when a child reaches two years of age and again at the end of the EYFS, essentially so that schools can report on children's progress to their parents.

Involving parents in assessment

Indeed, although reporting to parents is a requirement in the EYFS, there should always be a virtuous circle of communication between the two (parents and schools) so that each informs the other about the child, when they are in their care. Research shows that involving parents at the start of a child's school life is easier than involving them later so if schools wish to keep parents engaged with children's schooling they should draw them in, right from the start of nursery or Reception class. The benefits of this approach can include building positive relationships between family members and school teams; involvement of families in school through attendance at events such as assemblies, sporting fixtures, celebrations and plays, accompanying trips or taking part in fund-raising events. When parents engage with schools in this way there is a certain amount of 'buy-in' to partnership working which can then be focused on children's learning. This can be extremely rewarding for parents as well as for teachers and school teams. Seeking parents' views about their children as learners is an excellent starting point for schools to show they value parents' knowledge of their own children and their opinions about their child's strengths and needs. How this is done is entirely a decision that each school will make, based on the neighbourhood, families and children they serve. However, consider each of the following to determine the levels of engagement you facilitate currently:

Table 4.1 Assessing levels of parental engagement

Type of activity	Established	Developing	On my radar	Something I should consider
Termly parents' evenings				
Drop-in sessions once a week during the day in the first term for parents to visit				
Half-termly stay and play sessions				
Termly stay and play sessions				
Annual stay and play sessions				
Parents sharing books or reading stories to their children				
Teachers sharing books or reading stories to children with parents attending				
Parents sharing skills with a class or groups of children, e.g. gardening, art or music				
Parents sharing information or talking about their own culture or way of life to class or groups of children, e.g. sharing food, talking about celebrations or bringing items for children to look at				

Type of activity	Established	Developing	On my radar	Something I should consider
Grandparents sharing information or talking about their own childhood to class or groups of children				
Parents attending class events, e.g. to watch an assembly each term				
Parents managing library book loans				
Parents donating, using, or returning books to a children's library run by parents for children				
Parents helping at events such as a Summer fair, Halloween disco, etc.				
School staff visiting children at home with their parents (if invited by parents to do so)				
Series of induction visits by parents or carers with child during school day				
Series of induction sessions for parents or carers without child during school day or evening to suit families				
Series of induction sessions for parents or carers with crèche for child(ren) during school day or evening to suit families				
EYFS space on school website containing practical information for parents such as what time school starts and ends, how to help their children as they start school, etc.				
Virtual tour of the EYFS on the school website showing the indoor and outdoor areas of the EYFS classes and examples of activities that children would enjoy, e.g. water play, block play, story sessions				

To decide on your current level of parental engagement identify one of the following:

- Mostly in 'Established': High level of engagement
- Mainly in 'Developing': Medium level of engagement
- Mainly in 'On my radar': Low level of engagement

If, after completing the matrix (Table 4.1) you have time, go to the 'Something I should consider' column and add notes that will help you continue to develop in this essential area.

Communicating effectively with parents is key to success in finding out about a child. Many parents have absolutely no concerns about their young children as they start in nursery or Reception classes, particularly as most children will already have attended part- or full-time provision for a considerable time before starting 'real' school. Having a very simple format for finding out from parents about their child is important. You might want to use an ice-breaker with a group of parents to get them feeling relaxed enough to talk about their own children.

One way is to get parents together (some may already know one another – if they do, that's all the better!) to write three words that describe their child. Then ask them to share their words with the group, before displaying all the words together on a whiteboard – showing that the list may range from mischievous to timid, quiet to noisy or happy to grumpy. The point of this exercise is to help parents to see that their own child may well share some characteristics with other children in the class and to let them know that it will be the school's job to meet all of their different needs so that they settle into school easily.

As parents develop trust in the adults they meet in school they will find it much easier to express any concerns about their child if they feel that they will be listened to and that the school will act upon their concerns, whatever these are. For example, sometimes parents worry about leaving their child at the start of the school year and their child may express anxiety at being left – inevitably the feelings of the parent will affect the child and vice versa – but if the parent is able to talk about this to the child's key worker there may be simple strategies that the parent and school can take to alleviate this situation. Similarly, parents may have concerns about their children's development in other domains such as their speech, ability to relate to others or in relation to their learning. Some of these issues may derive from parents' ideas about what their child 'should' be doing in these areas, rather than being focused on what their child can do. However, parents are usually accurate in assessing their children's level of development, particularly if the child is not the only child in a family. This is particularly important if a parent believes their child has an additional need, which is why it is essential to take such views seriously. It is therefore critical to provide parents with both verbal and written information to help them understand their children's developmental journey. Look at Table 4.2 and identify which of the following things you provide (or could offer) to support parents in this area.

Table 4.2 Information to parents

Type of information provided	Established	Developing	On my Radar	Something I should consider
Reference copy of 'What to expect, when? Guidance to your child's learning and development in the EYFS' (4Children Publication)				
Physical activity guidelines for early years (under 5s) for children who are capable of walking (DoH)				
Early Years Outcomes (2013)				
Special educational needs and disability: A guide for parents and carers (DfE, 2014)				
Simple guide to CoEL				
Contact numbers for speech and language therapists, health visitors, etc.				
Copies of the class rules for behaviour				
Information about services at the local children's centre				
Details of how to seek advice and guidance from the school SENCO				
Leaflets providing advice about sleep, toilet training, the use of dummies, behaviour management, etc.				

If you offer all or most of the above, the likelihood is that your school is very positive with parents who have concerns about their children's development. When relationships with schools are good, parents do not normally feel threatened about sharing their concerns; when relationships are not so well-developed, distance can be created between the family and the school which is counter-productive, so it's important that adults involved in the EYFS should be prepared to listen respectfully to parents so that their concerns are understood and addressed as far as possible. Jotting down brief notes when this happens can be helpful so that the situation can be reviewed regularly and the parent can be updated and supported at all times.

A further action could be creating a 'next steps' plan for the child with the parent, recognising that the needs of the whole child are paramount as far as a child's education is concerned so, for example, if a parent is concerned that their child is not eating their lunch, the school should recognise that this is an area which, whilst at one level not necessarily having an observable effect on the child's learning, would be important because of what it represents in relation to their overall health and wellbeing. Therefore, it is imperative to work with the family to help the child feel safe and secure in the setting so that they enjoy eating at lunchtime.

Orienting ourselves on the unique pathway of each child's development

What has been discussed so far in this chapter is assessment, which is the way we shine a light on each unique child to know and understand them better for the people they are. Because young children are people – people with a variety of experiences and a view of the world that is very different from that of adults – it is important that we learn about them in order to know them better, orienting ourselves on their unique learning and developmental pathways.

Beginning by developing relationships of trust with them and their parents, schools create a picture of each child through on-entry assessment which is based on observations and is informed by what has been shared by parents, preschool providers and sometimes by other professionals such as a speech and language therapist (SALT). Using this multi-dimensional information can help to inform teachers' thinking about ways to support each child to enjoy their time in school, to benefit from a new range of experiences and to make progress in their learning and development. To find each child's future trajectory we need to spend time with them, talk to them, play alongside them and build a clear view of the ways they learn and the things that interest them and then consider how we can engage them in taking the next steps in their learning and development. This approach creates a bridge from the things the child knows and can do towards what the child will be able to do and learn next and is substantially different from an approach which simply identifies gaps to fill in the child's knowledge, learning or skills.

The subtlety of this difference is in the way the child is constructed in each approach: either as a competent learner (as in the EYFS) or as a vessel to be filled (an outdated model). In the EYFS, the task of teachers is to ensure that all sources of information, including what is learned directly from children, are brought together in developing an appropriate curriculum for each child.

By analysing findings from on-entry observational assessments, schools can consider ways to offer children with the same interests and developmental needs similar experiences. For example, thinking about physical development: moving and handling, it might be that many of the youngest children in a Reception class would need more opportunities for developing gross motor skills such as engaging in pushing toy cars around a large tuff tray, sweeping soapy water along a path or waving flags at the start and end of a series of bike races. Whilst, older or more mature children might benefit from activities that strengthened their wrists and elbows such as painting at an easel, screwing and unscrewing wooden nuts and bolts in a construction set or setting up and playing with puppets in a table-top theatre. Or, some children might need lots of opportunities for moving safely around the environment, or balancing and getting down safely from equipment. Simply by finding out what children can do already schools are able to plan experiences and activities that will meet the needs of the majority of children in different areas or aspects of learning. Setting these as next steps which are communicated to all staff members, parents and the child immediately prioritises these on everybody's agenda.

Ongoing assessment helps us to support learning

As we get to know children and identify their next steps for learning, ongoing assessment is used by skilful practitioners to adjust their interactions with children in order to take account of their different responses. Take for example, Tom who is, according to his parents, 'obsessed with firefighting' because his aunt and uncle are both fire fighters. During the spring term when a visit from the Fire Service has been planned to focus on understanding the world: people and communities, the teacher knows that Tom will be all too familiar with much of what the children will learn on the day of the visit so plans to spend more time with Tom beforehand so that they can explore some of the things he doesn't yet know about the work of the Fire Service, such as the number of fire fighters in a crew, the names of different vehicles used by the Fire Service, or the length of each 'watch' and the number of 'watches' in a day. The teacher might also help children like Tom to focus on the similarities and differences between services such as the Police and Fire Service. By building on initial plans for all of the children, the teacher can make Tom's (and other children's) experiences equally rewarding using ongoing assessment to differentiate the outcome from the visit.

Using this approach ensures children's needs for novelty and stimulation are met because each child is offered experiences that extend their skills, challenge their thinking and inspire their engagement. This way of teaching focuses on what the child can do and is interested in, in order to 'scaffold' the child's learning through timely and contingent interaction so that they are enabled to reach a different stage in their learning. Because this way of working is commonplace in early years classrooms teachers often underestimate their skills in this area, believing that the decisions they make are simply 'common sense'. Consider the following two examples:

Example 1

A TA takes a group of four children to a tuff tray, which contains straw, sticks, plastic bricks, three pigs, a wolf and copies of a story map. The learning intentions for the activity she has been directed to include:

- I can retell a part of the story using props (Low challenge)
- I can retell a simple story using props (Medium challenge)
- I can retell a simple story using a story map (Higher challenge)

One child immediately begins by saying 'I can do this without stopping' and in one breath retells the story rapidly, pointing in turn to each of the pictures on the story map. The TA recognises that the child retold the story (even though that was not how she had anticipated it would be done) and is very positive with the child, telling them that they have done 'a good job'. She then asks the child if they could help to support two of the children who are going to retell the story using props ('making sure they don't leave out any important bits'), so that she can work with the child who is retelling only a part of the story. In this way the TA has used ongoing assessment to make a judgement about a child's current learning and by tasking the child with ensuring the other two children do an accurate recall is cleverly extending demand on the child's listening and attention skills.

Example 2

A teacher is working with a group of children who are deciding what prices to charge in a café they have set up, following a visit to a café at a local park. Recognising that their knowledge of money is very scant the teacher suggests that no item on the café menu should cost more than ten pence and most children busily begin to say numbers between one and ten for the teacher to add to price tags for the café. But one child says that bottles of water should be 'twenty hundred' and another child says they should be 'five quid'. Once the prices are agreed (between one and ten pence) and the price tags are

A café or shop may be set up following a visit in the locality

in place most of the children are delighted to begin to sell items, spending real money. This satisfies everybody except the child who had suggested the price of 'twenty hundred' so the teacher begins to explore with the child why this amount was so important to them. From this emerges the fact that the child has heard an older sibling counting aloud from ten to a hundred and is only able to remember the second and last numbers in the string: 'twenty' and a 'hundred'. Using this information, the teacher is able to show the child how the numbers twenty and a hundred are part of a string of words used to count in tens. She then introduces Numicon™ blocks to show the child that counting in tens can be quicker than counting in single units. This exploration instantly motivates the child to practise saying the words, 'Ten, twenty, thirty…' Delighted that their contribution to the discussion has been valued by the teacher the child then shortly joins in with the rest of the group. Meanwhile, the teacher turns her attention to the task of exploring the other child's understanding of 'five quid', again using ongoing assessment to make decisions about how to support the child's learning.

It may appear that neither of the examples are about assessment yet both examples illustrate *'ongoing assessment (also known as formative assessment)* [which] *is an integral part of the learning and development process. It involves practitioners observing children to understand their level of achievement, interests and learning styles, and to then shape learning experiences for each child reflecting those observations'* (DfE, 2017:13). Clearly, this method of assessment requires adults to be on hand and receptive to children's thinking and understanding and also aware of any misapprehensions they may have, which demands significant skill if teaching is to be focused accurately for each child.

Summative assessment: Reflecting on what we know about each child

There are two fixed summative assessment points in the EYFS: one during the child's third year and another at the end of the EYFS. Detailed reference to the first of these, the two-year-old assessment, is likely to be relevant only for children entering nursery whose development is below the age-related expectation of between 22 to 36 months or 30 to 50 months (dependent on the child's chronological age on entry to nursery), for children below 30 to 50 months, or those with additional needs or disabilities entering Reception classes. In either case, where a child's development is not in line with their age, these areas should be identified and strategies put in place to support their needs accordingly. In its guidance to parents, the DfE indicates: *'If your child has a disability, whether or not they have SEN, their school must make reasonable adjustments, including the provision of auxiliary aids (such as tactile signage or induction loops) and services to prevent them being put at a substantial disadvantage'* (DfE, 2014:30).

The same document continues by informing parents:

'SEN support can take many forms. This could include:

- *a special learning programme for your child*
- *extra help from a teacher or a learning support assistant*
- *making or changing materials and equipment*
- *working with your child in a small group*
- *observing your child in class or at break and keeping records*
- *helping your child to take part in the class activities*
- *making sure that your child has understood things by encouraging them to ask questions and to try something they find difficult*
- *helping other children to work with your child, or play with them at break time*
- *supporting your child with physical or personal care difficulties, such as eating, getting around school safely, toileting or dressing'* (DfE, 2014:30).

Clearly, if in spite of the necessary adjustments being made the child does not make progress or your school is unable to offer appropriate provision, then you would need to involve the parents and representatives such as the SENCO from your school, in consideration of whether a child might need an EHC plan. This would involve further professional assessments of the child's needs and the nature of support necessary would be considered by a multi-professional team. Decisions would be made about where such provision might be offered – either in your school or within another.

The second assessment point is at the end of the EYFS, when it is a statutory requirement that schools (and settings) complete the EYFS Profile for children in Reception classes (or preschools) through assessing the extent to which they have achieved each of the ELGs, which *'summarise the knowledge, skills and understanding that all young children should have gained by the end of the Reception year'* (DfE, 2017:10). How information about each child's *'knowledge, skills and understanding'* is gathered is the responsibility of each school since the EYFS Profile Guidance states: *'In the context of statutory teacher assessment, it is a setting's own assessment policy which forms the basis of a practitioner's judgements about what children know and can do. This will provide the evidence upon which practitioners make a judgement against the ELGs as set out in the EYFS profile'* (STA, 2018:11).

In effect, teachers teach and gather evidence of the extent to which their teaching has been successful in helping children to meet each of the 17 outcomes (ELGs) set out in the EYFS. The way these are categorised ranges from the 'expected' level which the majority of children are likely to achieve at the end of the EYFS against the exceeding and emerging levels – self-explanatory terms accounting for the remaining numbers of children who will be deemed to be 'above' or 'not yet reaching' the expected level. In itself this explanation works to some degree, yet when we consider the age range of children at the end of the EYFS the likelihood is that the top and bottom end of the curve will be filled with mainly older or younger children. This age difference is brought home very strongly when I recall members of the second class I taught. In it were three brothers (all in the same year group): the oldest, whose birthday was in September, and his identical twin siblings, born the following August (when their older brother was 11 months old and could probably walk and communicate quite effectively)! This is a factor that is very significant when analysing outcomes. However, as always, schools should be vigilant about identifying children's additional needs as early as possible in order to intervene sooner so that every child has the required support if they struggle to keep up with their peers.

Each school's assessment policy details how teacher assessment will be carried out, recognising that the guidance states: *'Most evidence for EYFS profile judgements will come from practitioners observing a child's self-initiated activities'* (STA, 2018:14). This is an all-important point that relates to the first sentence in this chapter which argued that when we assess less and teach more, children learn better. Undoubtedly, this approach may not be favoured by all assessment leaders because of the many pressures placed on schools to be accountable for ensuring that all children make progress and that no child is left behind. Yet, although it may be counter-intuitive to 'assess less', it is likely that when this is the case children will achieve more because teaching will be more accurately focused on their learning needs. Whereas, in schools where for assessment purposes every child in the school must, for example, complete a piece of writing every two weeks, it is important to question whether this is this a good use of time. Indeed, research evidence suggests that when children found an activity to be *'enjoyable and satisfying'* they experienced *'greater motivation than those who received rewards from other people'* (Burnett, D., 2017). In other words, intrinsic motivation was found to be more of a motivator than when children were told they would be rewarded for engaging in an activity (in this case, playing with colourful art materials). The moral of this seems to be that if we want children to engage in any area of learning we should not demotivate them by offering extrinsic rewards. Rather, we should delight in their inner desire to pursue their own interests, the outcomes of which are more likely to represent their learning more accurately than what is created as part of an 'assessment' process.

Key takeaway

Obviously, there is a balance to be struck between finding out what children know, can do and understand and spending time on gathering evidence through adult-led activities. Utilising some opportunities to allow children to demonstrate their learning is perfectly acceptable since this is about enabling a child to show what they know or can do and is distinct from setting up situations that test a child's learning, such as asking a child to complete a worksheet. This is highlighted in the EYFS Profile which states: *'Practitioners' assessments are primarily based on observing a child's daily activities and events. In particular, practitioners should note the learning which a child demonstrates spontaneously, independently and consistently in a range of contexts'* (STA, 2018:6).

Consider the different approaches in Table 4.3 to assessing children's learning and identify the range of approaches you employ in your school and your rationale for each.

Table 4.3 Approaches to assessing children's learning and development

Type of assessment	Yes	No	Rationale
Planned ongoing observational assessment of individuals			
Planned ongoing observational assessment of groups			
Specific activities planned to allow children to demonstrate learning, e.g. inviting children to retell a story with puppets			
Spontaneous observations in continuous provision, e.g. a piece of writing, a conversation on the phone			
Fixed, teacher-led assessment points throughout the year to find out about aspects of a child's progress			
Discussions with a child to identify skills, knowledge and understanding			
Regular meetings with staff team to assess children's learning			
Inviting more and less able children to work together on a shared task such as giving out the fruit at snack time			
Inviting particular children to answer specific questions (rather than choosing children randomly)			
Inviting children to share their learning during a plenary session			

When you have completed Table 4.3 you may wish to consider which types of assessment are in keeping with the principles of the EYFS, bearing in mind the importance of a child demonstrating learning *spontaneously, independently and consistently in a range of contexts.*

The EYFS also sets out the parameters of effective learning, stating that this is shaped by the three characteristics (referred to also in Chapter 2): play and exploration (engagement), active learning (motivation) and creating and thinking critically (thinking). Referring to Table 4.4, identify where you have planned for children to demonstrate these characteristics.

Table 4.4 Opportunities for demonstrating the characteristics of effective learning

Playing and Exploring (Engagement)	Active Learning (Motivation)	Creating and Thinking Critically (Thinking)
Being Curious	**Being Focused**	**Thinking for themselves**
Activities/Experiences	Activities/Experiences	Activities/Experiences
Pretending	**Trying hard**	**Being a detective**
Activities/Experiences	Activities/Experiences	Activities/Experiences
Having a go	**Being proud when they tried to...**	**Finding a new way to do something**
Activities/Experiences	Activities/Experiences	Activities/Experiences

If you have found that you do plan to provide opportunities for children to demonstrate these aspects of their learning, you may wish to consider whether your ongoing assessments might be further extended (or started, if you don't plan for these) by use of the observational tool (Table 4.5).

Table 4.5 Observational tool for Characteristics of Effective Learning

Playing and Exploring (Engagement)	Active Learning (Motivation)	Creating and Thinking Critically (Thinking)
I saw you: Being curious...	**I saw you:** Being focused...	**I saw you:** Thinking for yourself...

Playing and Exploring (Engagement)	Active Learning (Motivation)	Creating and Thinking Critically (Thinking)
I saw you: Pretending to…	I saw you: Trying hard…	I saw you: Being a detective…
I saw you: Having a go…	I saw you: Being proud when you tried to…	I saw you: Finding a new way to do something…

The importance of the above characteristics cannot be overstated since as part of the statutory reporting requirements (to Year One teachers and to parents) schools must provide, in addition to a written summary of each child's attainment against the 17 ELGs, *'a short commentary on how* [each] *child demonstrates the 3 characteristics of effective learning'* (STA, 2018:25). The purpose of this statement is explained especially in relation to children whose achievements, in the early learning goals (ELGs) at the end of the EYFS, are considered to be 'emerging' or *'not yet at the level of development expected at the end of the EYFS'* when *'conversations between EYFS and year 1 staff* [should be] *meaningful so that the child makes a successful transition'* (STA, 2018:15).

Transition is discussed more fully in Chapter 9. However, it is fair to say that if schools create the right conditions for learning beyond the EYFS, teaching becomes part of a journey of discovery and can be focused on the needs of each child. And, by engaging more with children in playful learning opportunities, teachers are enabled to teach more accurately and children are enabled to learn better – a win-win situation.

It is well worth considering how parents of children feel at this time when a professional confers with them about their child's development. For parents whose children achieve in line with the expectations (expected) their responses are likely to be positive. And, those parents too whose children achieve beyond the expectations at the exceeding level (N.B. the EYFS is not weighted for age) are likely to feel positive. If, however, for some reason their child is deemed to not be achieving at either of these levels and their development is considered to be 'emerging', this may be unnerving and worrying for parents, hence the importance of the narrative around the CoEL: how children learn. The latter should identify the child's attitudes and dispositions to learning in an upbeat way so that parents recognise the ways in which their child is learning.

Finally, where a child is deemed to have a special need your school SENCO should support you to develop an annual report on the child's progress. And together with parents, you should talk at least three times a year about the child's progress, setting clear outcomes, alongside notes about the action taken and support agreed. Obviously, this will vary from school to school. Understanding this support and action will allow parents to recognise and celebrate the vast array of things that their child can do which is what all skilful educators focus on when assessing children's learning.

Sources

Statutory framework for the early years foundation stage: Setting the standards for learning, development and care for children from birth to five (2017)

'The EYFS specifies requirements for learning and development and for safeguarding children and promoting their welfare. The learning and development requirements cover:

- the areas of learning and development which must shape activities and experiences (educational programmes) for children in all early years settings
- the early learning goals that providers must help children work towards (the knowledge, skills and understanding children should have at the end of the academic year in which they turn five)
- assessment arrangements for measuring progress (and requirements for reporting to parents and/or carers).' (Page 5)

'The EYFS seeks to provide:

- **partnership working** between practitioners and with parents and/or carers
- **a secure foundation** through learning and development opportunities which are planned around the needs and interests of each individual child and are assessed and reviewed regularly.' (Page 5)

'In planning and guiding children's activities, practitioners must reflect on **the different ways that children learn** and reflect these in their practice. Three characteristics of effective teaching and learning are:

- playing and exploring – children investigate and experience things, and 'have a go'
- active learning – children concentrate and keep on trying if they encounter difficulties, and enjoy achievements

- creating and thinking critically – children have and develop their own ideas, make links between ideas, and develop strategies for doing things.' (Page 10)

DFE (2014) Special educational needs and disability: A guide for parents and carers

'If your child has a disability, whether or not they have SEN, their school must make reasonable adjustments, including the provision of auxiliary aids (such as tactile signage or induction loops) and services to prevent them being put at a substantial disadvantage. Schools also have wider duties to prevent discrimination, to promote equality of opportunity and to foster good relations.'

'If you think your child has SEN or a disability, you should talk to your school – start with the class teacher. Every school has to have a teacher who co-ordinates the SEN provision in the school called a SENCO (see Glossary) and you might also need to talk to them.'

'If your child's school thinks your child has SEN, they should talk to you to see what you think and gather evidence such as reports about your child's progress. If they decide to provide your child with support for their SEN, they must tell you.'

'If your child has SEN, your school needs to use its best endeavours – that means to do its very best – to give your child the support they need. That could include getting advice and support from specialists outside the school (such as an educational psychologist, a speech and language therapist or a specialist teaching and advisory service). Children with SEN will be provided with SEN support (see section in this guide on Support for children and young people with special educational needs).'

'The support provided is to help children achieve the outcomes or learning objectives that have been set for them.

SEN support can take many forms. This could include:

- a special learning programme for your child
- extra help from a teacher or a learning support assistant
- making or changing materials and equipment
- working with your child in a small group
- observing your child in class or at break and keeping records
- helping your child to take part in the class activities
- making sure that your child has understood things by encouraging them to ask questions and to try something they find difficult
- helping other children to work with your child, or play with them at break time
- supporting your child with physical or personal care difficulties, such as eating, getting around school safely, toileting or dressing.'

'Your child's school must provide you with an annual report on your child's progress. They should talk to you regularly about your child's progress, (at least three times a year), set clear outcomes and produce a report of these as well as the action taken and support agreed, and you may want to ask for this to be outside of the regular parents' evening. It's important that the views of your child are included in these discussions.

If the school, despite its best endeavours, can't meet your child's needs then you should consider whether your child might need an Education, Health and Care (EHC) needs assessment which might lead to an EHC plan (see section in this guide on Education, Health and Care needs assessments and plans). You should discuss this with your child's school (your child's class teacher or the school's SENCO).' (Pages 30–31)

STA (2018) Early years foundation stage profile handbook

'Adult-led activities can offer insight into children's attainment by making sure the child has the opportunity to demonstrate what they know, understand and can do.' (Page 14)

5 Starting with the child: Planning from children's interests

Key Points

- Be confident that given the right opportunities children will be able to lead their own learning
- Capitalise on teachable moments when they occur and don't put things off till later
- Cast a wide net to find and follow children's interests and schema
- Support children to believe in themselves as 'experts' in certain areas

The whole focus of this chapter is around self-belief: children's self-belief and teachers' self-belief. Henry Ford's much quoted saying is one I often refer to in discussions with teachers both in relation to their own skills and abilities and in relation to children: 'Whether you think that you can, or that you can't, you are usually right' (i newspaper: 27th October 2017). This refers to one of the most important human characteristics – describing a sense of agency or competence that is so powerful that it takes people much further than almost any other trait. One of the first things that I tell teachers is to be confident that children will be able to lead their own learning. Why? Because the key to learning is motivation and when children set their hearts on doing something they are likely to strive much more than if the task is one set by somebody else (no matter how well meaning that person is).

Children leading their own learning

> ### CASE STUDY: ROAD BRIDGES
>
> The following case study is drawn from a school where I supported developments in the EYFS. It is about three boys playing together, in the outside area of a Reception class, and illustrates this point.
>
> The boys had some toy cars and two pieces of guttering resting on one another and on to a tyre. They appeared to be throwing cars haphazardly into the guttering. Indeed because of the way they were doing this a Teaching Assistant (TA) made his way over to them to try to redirect what appeared to be their 'off-task' behaviour.

However, satisfying himself that he had told them to stop 'throwing' he moved away, directing his attention elsewhere. After this, the boys resumed throwing the cars and I continued observing them for a few more moments before realising why they needed to throw them. Their lack of success was because the two pieces of guttering didn't fit together. What the boys were trying to do, I realised, was to get the cars past the break in the guttering and into the second part of the 'run' so that they would speed down the other side. That this was an impossibility was not obvious to Muhammad, Arlo and Luca; nor did they realise that their efforts would never pay off. Helping them to solve this problem became the focus of another adult and, after some discussion, the boys were soon gathering wooden blocks to build under their road bridge so that the guttering would become level with the height of the tyre and then the break between the gutter sections would no longer matter. And, indeed, after they did this there was no longer a gap between the sections so the cars could now run along the channel and down the other side of the tyre.

The important message from this scenario is that whilst the situation enabled the children to lead their own learning what was missing initially was the 'correct' input. The response of the TA may be explained by the fact that he believed that the boys' behaviour was inappropriate, particularly since I was observing practice in the EYFS Unit. His focus on behaviour is easily understood but had he had the confidence to analyse what was happening, he might have helped the boys to reach different conclusions about the problem they had encountered. Whilst the conditions and resources for learning were present, on their own, they were not sufficient until the teaching focused on what the children were trying to achieve. In this case, it was a happy accident that changed the outcome because the new adult became an enabling partner in their play, understanding their frustration and also recognising the importance of allowing them to talk their problem through. They knew what they wanted to achieve but needed a 'more capable other' to help them develop their thinking so that they could solve the problem.

Capitalising on teachable moments

Teaching young children is, to a large extent, about the factors that encourage interaction and which lead to episodes of shared thinking. In many ways Ofsted is helpful in identifying that: 'Teaching in the early years should not be taken to imply a 'top down' or formal way of working. It is a broad term that covers the many different ways in which adults help young children learn. It includes their interactions with children during planned and child-initiated play and activities: communicating and modelling language, showing, explaining, demonstrating, *exploring ideas, encouraging, questioning, recalling, and providing a narrative for what they are doing, facilitating and setting challenges'* (Ofsted, 2016:58). And, although this description is by no means complete, it can help us to think about the ways that children learn and to consider how we use different approaches in facilitating and enabling their learning through what are often referred to as 'teachable moments'. An adult being there at the right moment can make the difference between a child's success at learning and a missed opportunity. Teachable moments occur as teachers, in their moment by moment encounters with children, make decisions about their learning. This means that whilst initial planning may have been focused on developing children's mathematical skills through, for example, a small world scenario instead of engaging in counting items, children begin to create narratives. Then the teacher simply follows the children's lead to extend this aspect of their learning.

CASE STUDY: LEMONADE

In the following case study, based in a nursery, consider how the adult engaged with the child in a teachable moment.

A four-year-old girl was busy pretending to prepare lemonade in a home corner, richly supplied with fresh fruit and vegetables which children were using in all sorts of ways. Some of the children had stripped the leaves from leeks and curled them round in bun tins as pretend cakes, others were sniffing broccoli or breaking a cauliflower into florets to make soup. One little girl, Anna, was pretending to make lemonade with a real lemon positioned over a jug but just as she pushed the lemon on to the top of the jug it fell to the bottom of the jug.

Amazed she looked at the jug, tipping it upside down to see if the lemon would fall out. Meanwhile, the adult watched for a moment, then paused, considering what she should do and how Anna would react to the surprising disappearance of the lemon. Skilfully encouraging Anna, the practitioner invited her to think of ways to extract the lemon from the jug where it was stuck. Shaking the jug only brought the lemon to the narrow neck at the top; pushing a spoon into the jug to lift the lemon out only increased the size of what had to be pulled through the neck of the jug. When Anna carefully inserted her fingers into the jug she was able to guide the lemon through the narrow opening at the top, grasping the lemon with her fingers, which finally found their way out, holding on to the lemon!

Throughout the period the adult's encouragement acted as a strong motivator for the child to succeed. Had the adult not held back, Anna might have been helped to solve this tricky problem much more quickly, which would have meant that the imaginary lemonade was ready for the party, but the teacher recognised that this was not the most important consideration and spent time encouraging Anna to succeed in solving the problem she had met. Once Anna was successful in pulling the lemon out, she immediately pushed it back into the jug to see if she could get it out again, which of course she did, having found the most effective method from having tried a number of other strategies!

By choosing this approach the practitioner was able to introduce words such as *narrow, stuck, squeeze, tight, wider, grip, hold,* and so on. This example of a teachable moment might not have happened had the practitioner intervened by 'helping' the child to successfully make her lemonade; yet, following a moment's reflection they chose to act on their instincts by encouraging Anna to find a way to get the lemon out of the jug herself. Scaffolding Anna's learning in this way enabled Anna to demonstrate different characteristics of learning such as 'finding ways to solve problems' and 'testing ideas'.

Reflect on your own practice by inviting a colleague to consider the quality of your teaching using the proforma in Table 5.1, drawn from the Ofsted definition of teaching, referred to earlier. After your colleague completes the column: 'What was observed' discuss together any developments, actions or recommendations for ways to enhance this vital area, focusing strongly on how you provide for children's interests.

Table 5.1 Observing teaching

A. What we are looking for: How adults...	What was observed	Developments, actions or recommendations
Interact with children in planned play and activities		
Interact with children in child-initiated play and activities		

Communicate and model language		
Show and explain		
Demonstrate and explore ideas		
Encourage		
Question		
Recall and provide a narrative for what children are doing		
Facilitate and set challenges		
B. What we are looking for	**What was observed**	**Developments, actions or recommendations**
Equipment provided and attention to the physical environment		

How adults assess what children know, understand and can do		
How adults take into account children's interests and dispositions to learn		
How adults use this knowledge of children to plan children's next steps in learning		

Finding and following children's interests and schema

Teachers often tell me, when I ask, that the children in their class are interested in a range of things including outdoor play, sand, water, blocks, play dough and role play. Yet, I invite them to go beyond these suggestions and think again about what preoccupies children and to consider what ideas and concepts children are really interested in. This often highlights the fact that although adults know a great deal about their classes, what they sometimes know less about is what children bring to school in the way of their own experiences and interests.

A discussion with a group of Reception children revealed that they were interested in the concept of shopping and cafés and had experiences of visiting supermarkets and fast food restaurants. Further conversations revealed that they had noticed transactions using cards as well as money and that several had scanned items at self-service tills. Arriving at this conclusion is the start of finding the interests of a group of children. Talking to their parents can also be useful since they can be helpful in providing information which children may not be able to explain, such as whether a firework display described by the child was in celebration of an event or whether it was something the child noticed when looking through the window. The most important sources of information about children's interests are the children themselves and their parents. We can elicit information from children's actions, by listening to them and by observing them. Parents too can be encouraged to share information about their children.

Ask the family

A good way of doing this is by encouraging parents to share information through a diary or through a private section on the school website or an app such as Tapestry™ – this is particularly helpful following breaks such as weekends or half term. Knowing that a child has successfully weighed fruit and vegetables in a supermarket or collected conkers and acorns from the park can provide important clues for teachers who want to build on these experiences by offering opportunities and resources for the child to expand their learning.

Resources at the ready

The next steps for planning based around these experiences will vary from child to child and class to class – some children may want to turn the role play area into a shop and when provided with real tins and packets (bought cheaply from supermarket basics) a whole new area of learning may emerge focusing on the use of money, packing and unpacking shopping trolleys and baskets, role playing a customer operating a self-service till or a till operator serving a customer at the checkout. Supporting children to to be imaginative allows them to replay scenarios from real life – such as being a grown up, or to enter imaginary worlds to find out what it feels like to be a superhero, for example. Exploring the world in this way is more meaningful for a child than expecting them to join in some experiences that are planned but which are not high on their agenda at that particular time.

For the child who has been gathering autumn finds in a bag, their fascination may be with the texture and feel of the items or the stories and factual information that they connect with them. Stories of squirrels collecting their store of food for autumn may inspire movement or schema related to enveloping or enclosure; or children might simply want to play with their finds – creating shapes, patterns and stories around them. Having a box of items at hand to support this is important. If a themed box isn't available, think about creating one for this focus containing things such as twigs, plasticine (for standing twigs in), shiny brown material, acorns, a small wheelbarrow, conkers, mulled wine spice sachets to bring a scent of autumn and soft toys (or small cast animal figures such as a squirrel, rabbit, fox). You could also include classic stories such as *The Tale of Squirrel Nutkin* by

Beatrix Potter, together with stories such as *The Busy Little Squirrel* by Nancy Tafuri, *Pumpkin Soup* by Helen Cooper or factual books about autumn. As interests develop and children's play goes off in different directions, develop more resource bags, boxes or suitcases to support their enquiries.

Supporting expertise

When we take time to listen to children we can often find that they have expertise in areas that we know little of. Examples of expertise will vary dependent on the area your school is in and the families you serve. However, you may find through talking to children that some young children in your class may well be experts in some of the following areas:

Table 5.2 Identifying children's expertise

Area of Interest	Child's initials	Area of Interest	Child's initials	Area of Interest	Child's initials
Gardening		Rugby		Cooking or baking	
The family pet		Swimming		Places such as beaches, caravan sites, campsites, other holiday destinations	
Fishing		Animals		Aeroplanes	
Minibeasts		Fairies		Shopping	
Dinosaurs		Disney characters		Transport	
TV programmes such as 'Paw Patrol' or 'X Factor'		Power Rangers		Caring for a baby or an elderly person	
Football		Superheroes		Apps such as Minecraft	
Trains		Gymnastics		Music	
Using a PC, laptop, smartphone or tablet		Telling stories		Ballet	
Local park		Soft play resource		Making things, e.g. Lego®	

You could create a table of your own and then add the initials of any children whose interests you have identified – this will allow you to decide on the type of resources you may need to gather, as well as to consider which adults may be available to support learning in these areas. In some cases, adults may need to brush up on their knowledge about fishing or football, for example, in order to be a resource for children!

Whatever area of expertise a child has, it is important to recognise that this is something that motivates them hugely and gives them both pleasure and satisfaction. A further benefit is that children's sense of self is enhanced just by having their expertise acknowledged which is, of course, the same for adults!

At one school I worked with, the EYFS leader was keen to develop the school's practice in supporting children's interests so they devised an observation sheet to identify the things children did when in child-initiated play and learning. The completed sheet looked like this:

Table 5.3 Children's Interests

Child's initials	Interests	Area of learning	Next step
MB MI	Painting using brushes and water on the walls and floor to make marks	Physical Development (PD) Writing (L)	Begin to form letters, shapes or symbols
GL LM	Using dumper trucks to role play	Expressive Arts and Design (EAD)	Introduce small world scene to extend role play – farm: hay, sawdust
AH AW	Naming and saying the sounds made by animals	Communication and Language (C&L)	Add to animal collection – varying to jungle animals for comparison
AS DLS GE	Playing scoring goals with footballs and net	Personal, Social and Emotional Development (PSED) Physical Development (PD)	Introduce simple team games to encourage cooperation
MC PC	Trying to use the pedals on a bike	Physical Development (PD)	Encouragement and one to one support to master this skill
GW PW FB MJ	Sensory play in the tuff tray using sawdust/hay-making and JB being farmer	Expressive Arts and Design (EAD) Communication and Language (C&L)	Introduce masks for storytelling to each other
HK RM	Lifting and dropping coins from different heights into water	Mathematical Development (MD)	Introduce deeper container and suggest different objects to experiment with

Interests observed

Particularly noticeable in their notes in Table 5.3 are the different types of schema that appeared in children's play. Therefore, the table below identifies some of the possible schema (column 1), describes these (column 2) and identifies the different activities undertaken by children which have been categorised accordingly (column 3). You will see that in some cases the same activity is shown in more than one place since the behaviours were illustrative of aspects of more than one schema.

Table 5.4 Schema observed

Schema type	Description	Schema noted
Enveloping or enclosure	Wrapping or enclosing items	Lifting and dropping coins from different heights into water Sensory play in the tuff tray using sawdust/hay-making and JB being farmer
Transporting	Moving items from one place to another	Using dumper trucks to role play
Trajectory	Projecting, directing or throwing items (balls, glitter or bean bags) or water, custard or other fluids (from hoses, taps or jugs)	Playing scoring goals with footballs and net Lifting and dropping coins from different heights into water
Rotational	Turning wheels, cogs or self-whirling ribbons, wind socks or self-twisting wires or strings	Trying to use the pedals on a bike
Vertical/Horizontal	Making stripes, tearing strips, mark making using up and down movements, creating ladders or lines of blocks	Painting using brushes and water on the walls and floor to make marks

Consider, for example the children playing in the water: were they exploring a vertical or horizontal schema by dropping coins from a height into water or were they more interested in thinking about the way the water enclosed the coins? Or think about the child interested in pedalling: would other observations show that they were intent on exploring a circular or rotational schema? So, when schema appear, they are worthy of serious consideration because of the insight they give into the child's development. For instance, if a child is interested in physically spinning around this may be their body's response to the need to develop their vestibular system, which occurs as the child moves and which controls 'posture, balance, alertness, concentration and stillness' (Connell, G. and McCarthy,

C., 2014:84) and without which the child would be unable to learn to sit still, ironic as this may sound! At the same time as this type of movement signals cues about the child's physical development, it also gives an insight into the child's conceptual development – a child's preoccupation with whirling round physically may also be connected with their understanding of rotation which may be noted in actions such as spinning coins, turning a musical tin or rolling a tyre. Concepts the child may gain through exploring such a schema are varied but might include understanding the difference between motion and movement or how light and heavy objects behave when they are moving.

The most important conclusion to draw from this very brief discussion of schema is that the child's actions are indicative of their physical and cognitive development, since the two are often inextricably linked as the brain lays down pathways of connections created by the physical experiences which are stored and called on in future action. This is an area that has been well documented elsewhere and is one that is worthy of further study in deciding what experiences are appropriate for three-, four- and five-year-olds in schools.

Key takeaway

To conclude this chapter, consider for the moment the following audit to decide if your current practice is:

a) providing children with plentiful opportunities to lead their own learning
b) allowing you to find and follow children's interests
c) helping you consider how you support children's expertise
d) enabling you to capitalise on teachable moments.

Highlight one box in each row in Table 5.5.

In judging your current approach, you may have found that whilst you don't write down planning around interests you do this from analysing observations. Clearly, that is perfectly acceptable, however you may find that you scored mainly in the 'on our radar' column and if this is the case the danger is that sometimes when something is only on the 'back burner' it can easily get overlooked – so do bear this in mind.

You have now considered some significant issues regarding what decisions you make about play, teaching and learning in your class and how this informs your decision-making. What you decide to do next is your choice. However, it is worth noting that planning from children's interests is a statutory requirement of the EYFS.

Table 5.5 Evaluating practice

Enabling children to lead their own learning			
Established	**Developing**	**On our radar**	**Something we should consider**
We plan flexibly to ensure that children have time to follow their interests	We sometimes plan flexibly to ensure that children have time to follow their interests	We occasionally plan flexibly to ensure that children have time to follow their interests	We rarely plan flexibly to ensure that children have time to follow their interests
We frequently amend planning to reflect the needs of different children	We sometimes amend planning to reflect the needs of different children	We occasionally amend planning to reflect the needs of different children	We rarely amend planning to reflect the needs of different children
Finding and following children's interests			
Established	**Developing**	**On our radar**	**Something we should consider**
We regularly consult with children about current interests	We sometimes consult with children about current interests	We occasionally consult with children about current interests	We rarely consult with children about current interests
We systematically consult with parents about their child's interests	We sometimes consult with parents about their child's interests	We occasionally consult with parents about their child's interests	We rarely consult with parents about their child's interests
We give regular electronic updates to parents about what their child is currently interested in at school	We sometimes give electronic updates to parents about what their child is currently interested in at school	We occasionally give electronic updates to parents about what their child is currently interested in at school	We rarely give electronic updates to parents about what their child is currently interested in at school
We frequently invite parents to share pictures of their child's interests at home	We sometimes invite parents to share pictures of their child's interests at home	We occasionally invite parents to share pictures of their child's interests at home	We rarely invite parents to share pictures of their child's interests at home
Capitalising on teachable moments			
Established	**Developing**	**On our radar**	**Something we should consider**
We always ensure that an adult is available to tune into children's interests and support their learning	We sometimes ensure that an adult is available to tune into children's interests and support their learning	We occasionally ensure that an adult is available to tune into children's interests and support their learning	We rarely ensure that an adult is available to tune into children's interests and support their learning

During observations we try to identify interests and note them down so that teaching can be more focused for each child	During observations we sometimes try to identify interests and note them down so that teaching can be more focused for each child	During observations we occasionally try to identify interests and note them down so that teaching can be more focused for each child	During observations we rarely identify interests and note them down so that teaching can be more focused for each child
Supporting children as experts			
Established	**Developing**	**On our radar**	**Something we should consider**
We frequently invite children to share their knowledge with small groups as well as the whole class	We sometimes invite children to share their knowledge with small groups as well as the whole class	We occasionally invite children to share their knowledge with small groups as well as the whole class	We rarely invite children to share their knowledge with small groups as well as the whole class
We always look for interesting resources to support children in their different areas of expertise	We sometimes look for interesting resources to support children in their different areas of expertise	We occasionally look for interesting resources to support children in their different areas of expertise	We rarely look for interesting resources to support children in their different areas of expertise

Sources of evidence

Ofsted school inspection handbook August 2018

'Inspecting the effectiveness of the early years provision: quality and standards

- how well teaching nurtures, engages and motivates children and promotes their sense of achievement and commitment to learning

- the breadth of the curriculum and how well it is based on accurate assessment of children's learning and development, so that activities and experiences meet their needs

- how well all staff work with parents, engage them in their children's learning and keep them informed about their children's achievements and progress

- children's enjoyment of learning, including their participation and willingness to make choices and decisions, and the extent to which children are active and inquisitive learners who are creative and think critically.' (Page 59)

Statutory framework for the early years foundation stage: Setting the standards for learning, development and care for children from birth to five (2017)

'Practitioners must consider **the individual needs, interests, and stage of development of each child** in their care, and must use this information to plan a challenging and enjoyable experience for each child in all of the areas of learning and development.' (Page 9)

Teachers' standards 2013

'Plan and teach well-structured lessons

- Promote **a love of learning** and children's intellectual curiosity

Adapt teaching to respond to the strengths and needs of all pupils

- **know when and how to differentiate appropriately**, using approaches which enable pupils to be taught effectively
- demonstrate an awareness of the physical, social and intellectual development of children, and know how to adapt teaching to support pupils' education at different stages of development.' (Page 8)

6 The environment for learning: Organising space and resources

Key Points

- Review how areas are used in your classroom and analyse why they are popular with some children (and why they aren't attracting other children)
- Carry out a cost/benefit analysis to inform your decisions about providing particular areas of provision
- Focus on making your space work successfully as an environment for play and learning
- Develop your unique selling point (USP) by identifying what makes your environment special

Taking time to stand back in a busy EYFS classroom can seem like an act of wilful negligence when there are so many compelling reasons young children would benefit from your attention at any one moment. Yet without taking some time to reflect on the organisation of space and resources in your classroom or unit, you could be missing vital clues about the focus of your teaching and of children's learning. In this chapter, we will explore how to judge whether the environment is fit for purpose so that an ongoing review of provision and resources becomes an integral part of decision-making in the EYFS.

The use, popularity and purpose of areas of provision

When I reflect on the resources and areas in EYFS classes I have visited over a number of years, I sometimes question the benefits of some of the items 'inherited' from predecessors. From unwanted sofas, armchairs, book boxes, bean bags, huge cushions and other items of furniture to those with missing handles, doors or hinges – these unwanted resources often land in schools and adults are sometimes too polite to refuse them! The first thing to consider is why certain items are taking up the space they do and whether they are worthwhile because unless the equipment and resources are appropriate for the needs of your class, it is hard to create a high-quality learning environment. Therefore, it is really useful to begin by auditing the environment to see which items warrant the space they take up and which aren't worth keeping. Another point to consider is the purpose of established areas and how these are being used by the children. It's worthwhile investing some time to find this out, because only by seeing what the children do in the areas can you judge whether the resources on offer are serving a useful purpose or not.

An area attracts children when it is well-maintained and inviting

Case study: Hot or cold: Use of the areas of provision

I spent some time in a nursery where take up of certain areas was strongly divided along gender lines: girls in some areas, boys in others. Although different areas were in use, competition for certain areas rivalled others, including a home corner, snack area, book area, sand/water and painting areas. Why, the teacher and I wondered, was this the case? There were many possible reasons such as a sudden interest in cards which could have appealed more to the girls who were in the mark-making area. Whilst the new and exciting enhancements in the block area might have had more appeal for boys, the only way of knowing was to understand the reasons why some areas seemed to be red 'hot' whilst others seemed stone 'cold', then to make a note of which children were using the areas and how they were using them.

In order to understand this, the teacher agreed to check throughout the day, recording the number of children entering and leaving the areas, as well as identifying what they were doing during this time.

A simple proforma was devised similar to Table 6.1, and notes were taken during any spare moments as the teacher taught in the continuous provision.

Table 6.1 Hot and cold spot observation

AREA	BOYS: 9.15 – 10.15	GIRLS: 9.15 – 10.15	BOYS: 10.30 – 11.30	GIRLS: 10.30 – 11.30	BOYS: 12.45 – 1.45	GIRLS: 12.45 – 1.45	BOYS:1.45 – 3.00	GIRLS: 1.45 – 3.00
Block play								
Home corner								
Sand								
Water								
Writing								
Making								
Book corner								
Snack								
Small world								
Painting								
Malleable								

Analysis of findings showed the 'hot' areas (the most popular areas) for boys were:

- Block play
- Sand area
- Water area

Whilst for girls the 'hot' spots were:

- Mark-making area
- Dough table (malleable area)
- Book corner

The 'cold' areas on the other hand were: the making area where it was noted that no child entered at any time, the home corner and painting area where only one or two girls showed any interest, and the small world area where several boys chose to play with the resources which linked to *Owl Babies* by Martin Waddell and Patrick Benson.

Examining these findings led to a consideration of adult involvement which, rather than being focused on managing learning, tended to be highly focused on managing resources instead. This meant that every adult was busy doing routine tasks, such as providing additional paper for children in the mark-making area, helping them fix their paper to the painting easel, or helping them to get ready for going out or to change their clothes when they came in from outside. The boys, who had chosen to play in the blocks, were left to get on by themselves. Similarly, the boys who played in the sand and water areas were also left to their own devices, as were the children who played in the malleable area, which was cramped and therefore not easy for an adult to get into. The conclusion was reached that because the boys seemed to be managing in the areas where they had chosen to spend their time the adults were seeking out tasks that made them look (and feel) 'busy'. This meant that the girls were 'rewarded' with more adult input than the boys – though this involvement focused mainly on managing their activity, rather than supporting their learning.

However, because adults were not engaged with the boys during these times opportunities were missed that might have extended their play and learning. So, how was the situation resolved in the school I have described and what lessons can be learned from their experience?

In this school it became a matter of focusing on children's needs and on the roles of adults in supporting children's play and learning. Clearly, many of the boys enjoyed being left to play uninterrupted alongside their peers, whilst the girls seemed to enjoy the comfort of being physically close to one another as they talked and played.

In all the areas which were 'hottest': block play, mark making and dough tables, the children were physically close to one another and they seemed to enjoy/need to be near the other children. As this scenario was observed in the autumn term, it is also fair to assume that their need for proximity to each other was related to their newness to the environment and that this would change as they gained confidence in this new space. However, it appeared that children were uncertain about separating from the group and were not yet at the stage where they could negotiate with friends to strike out and explore new areas.

To remedy this, it was agreed that the key person for each group would show photos (on their tablets) of the 'cold' areas to the children as they were deciding where to play so that these areas would become 'visible', rather than 'invisible places' which children had not considered. It was also agreed that adults would spend more time helping children to visit areas by introducing them to one area at a time in their key groups. A further decision was that there should be some sort of stimulus in areas so that children could get ideas for what they might do in them, such as in the making area or the malleable area. These stimuli are sometimes described as 'fascination traps' or 'provocations for learning', or as 'hooks' to invite children in. However, at this stage, our intention was merely to invite children to try out some of the tools and materials that they might not otherwise engage with. Setting up some of these incentives was effective and, as a result, the picture changed quickly so that groups of children tried out different areas. The result was that some 'cold' spots became 'hot' spots and other areas, such as the blocks area, became free for other children to try out.

Two further issues remained – both concerned the roles and responsibilities of adults in children's learning. It was agreed that adults should be there primarily to support children emotionally as they got to know, what must have seemed to them, the vast spaces (in and out of doors). Next it was decided that adults would role model, explain and demonstrate what could be done in a particular area so that children understood the possibilities and expectations of play in each area. This is because, in reality, areas of provision are simply a means by which adults create a backdrop to facilitate children's play. This may mean that only by sowing the seeds of what could happen, for example modelling how to role play the making of a meal in the home corner or the creation of a robot in the making area (not for children to copy slavishly but to help them develop their own ideas), can children know what sorts of things can be done in certain areas of provision.

Making decisions about which areas of provision to offer

What should be in an EYFS classroom? Why is this such a difficult question? Well, in one sense it isn't very difficult because most people seem to have the answer to it, since what is provided in an EYFS classroom or unit is not prescribed and is therefore a teaching decision. When I visit EYFS classes, units or learning environments I usually find that similar areas to those listed in Table 6.1 are present, though this is not an exhaustive list. In reality everybody is right and whatever the learning environment is like, so long as it enables the educational programmes set out in the EYFS (2017) to take place, nobody is wrong.

The EYFS states:

'*Educational programmes must involve activities and experiences for children, as follows:*

- **Communication and language** *development involves giving children opportunities to experience a rich language environment; to develop their confidence and skills in expressing themselves; and to speak and listen in a range of situations*

- **Physical development** *involves providing opportunities for young children to be active and interactive; and to develop their co-ordination, control, and movement. Children must also be helped to understand the importance of physical activity, and to make healthy choices in relation to food*

- **Personal, social and emotional development** *involves helping children to develop a positive sense of themselves, and others; to form positive relationships and develop respect for others; to develop social skills and learn how to manage their feelings; to understand appropriate behaviour in groups; and to have confidence in their own abilities*

- **Literacy** *development involves encouraging children to link sounds and letters and to begin to read and write. Children must be given access to a wide range of reading materials (books, poems, and other written materials) to ignite their interest*

- **Mathematics** *involves providing children with opportunities to develop and improve their skills in counting, understanding and using numbers, calculating simple addition and subtraction problems; and to describe shapes, spaces, and measure*

- **Understanding the world** *involves guiding children to make sense of their physical world and their community through opportunities to explore, observe and find out about people, places, technology and the environment*

- **Expressive arts and design** *involves enabling children to explore and play with a wide range of media and materials, as well as providing opportunities and encouragement for sharing their thoughts, ideas and feelings through a variety of activities in art, music, movement, dance, role-play, and design and technology*' (DfE, 2017:8–9).

From this, it is plain that the play opportunities we make available in the EYFS are largely down to professional judgement, based on principles within the EYFS, which are, of course, statutory and can be founded on any preferred philosophy such as Montessori, High Scope or those which I have discussed in a previous publication (Langston, A., 2014).

Other factors which may influence provision are:

a) funding which impacts not only on resources but also on ratios

b) whether there is access to a suitable outdoor area

c) whether staffing allows for good quality indoor and outdoor provision.

Creating the optimum environment for play and learning

Put simply, the optimum environment for learning is one in which the children thrive and the adults who work within it enjoy teaching and learning with the children. The direction of travel in terms of learning is broadly outlined in the EYFS – set out as Early Learning Goals to be achieved at the end of children's time in the Reception class of school. However, the EYFS is a framework and not a curriculum *per se* and therefore the curriculum is something that professionals are able to develop, provided they keep in sight the long-term goals that are set out in the EYFS. Therefore, whilst music might be a particular area of interest in a school, it would not be sufficient to teach this to the exclusion of everything else since this would almost certainly lead to a narrowness which might mean that children missed out on other things, such as exploring relationships with others or enjoying stories. Admittedly, this is an extreme example though, even on its own music might tick a lot of boxes in relation to learning in the EYFS! However, if we are to provide fully for children we need to be clear about the importance of a broad curriculum and how we offer it to children.

An area inviting children to explore and find out

How do we know if we have created the optimum environment for play and learning in our EYFS class or unit? In order to do this, we can consider how we expect children to develop in the way that the EYFS prescribes. Begin, for example, by thinking about how you support some of the skills children are expected to achieve in the three prime areas in Table 6.2. You may wish to jot down where and when these opportunities occur in your setting – if these are planned over a period of time your environment will reflect this. If this is not the case then it may be worth exploring why this is so.

Table 6.2 Skills: C&L, PD and PSED

C&L	Where and when?	PD	Where and when?	PSED	Where and when?
Listening		Developing control		Developing confidence	
Responding		Developing co-ordination		Exploring and finding out	
Questioning		Developing movement skills		Developing self-help skills	
Commenting		Handling tools		Developing Independence	
Following instructions		Handling equipment		Expressing feelings, opinions and ideas	
Answering questions		Handling writing tools		Taking turns; sharing and getting along with others	
Expressing themselves		Understanding why we exercise		Learning to adapt behaviour and negotiate with others	
Talking about events		Knowing ways to keep safe		Understanding that different people make choices of their own	
Developing narratives		Knowing ways to keep healthy		Adjusting behaviour in different situations	
Explaining				Forming positive relationships	

In order to support children developing the skills (in column one of Table 6.2), it is clearly important that they have opportunities to listen, talk and interact with others. This suggests that even in a busy environment, children should be able to hear and listen to each other and to adults, yet many classrooms are noisy and this can present problems for adults and children alike. Yet when teachers focus on reducing noise by asking children to use quiet voices, it can be reduced significantly – so much so, that it is often then the adults who need reminding to use their quiet voices!

It is important, too, to bear in mind that in order to talk about events and to express themselves well children need a variety of first-hand experiences that are meaningful for them. It may be that having a family member attend a stay and play session is a really important event to one child, whilst observing a duck egg hatching out might be more significant to another child – whatever the motivator we should provide it so that children are both willing and eager to reflect on their experiences and share their thoughts. Adults should also have the skills to extend children's talk and thinking through using skilful strategies that support memory and recall of events. These might include prompting the child to remember an event such as when they acted a part in the nativity play or climbed up to reach a branch on a tree, or it might involve helping them recall a process such as how they made a robot from junk or a den from material, pegs and tape.

In order to develop the physical skills that underpin all future development children need space to move in and experiences that will allow them to develop both gross (large movements – such as walking and running) and fine (small movements – such as pointing and tapping) motor skills. In order to develop these skills children need sustained and frequent opportunities to explore a range of materials including dough, paper, water, sand, as well as to use items such as scissors, staplers, spoons, forks, paint brushes, wheeled toys and the like.

We know that only by moving around do children develop the capacity to sit still for short periods of time, so again this is something that should inform your thinking when you plan the environment. Consider whether you are brave enough to have a movement mat where children can go and stretch out and move when they need to, or is this sort of activity confined to PE or outdoor play opportunities?

In Table 6.2 interpersonal skills (relationships and self-regulation) are high priority areas. It is important to take into account that these skills are taught, rather than caught and that they do not just 'happen', nor should we expect them to do so. Again, the younger the child, the more adults will need to understand their responses since young children's emotions are very close to the surface. In the face of not wanting to share or conform to some other expectation, children often need help to deal with their instincts and emotions. In addition, the younger the child the more that warm interaction and positive relationships are fundamental to their wellbeing.

These prime areas of the EYFS are the very ones from which the specific areas develop. Without communication skills there is little appreciation of rhyme, sound or narrative; without social skills there can be little understanding of the world and without some physical skills there can be little awareness of the body and fewer ways of responding to art, music or experience.

Below are two of the specific areas of the EYFS, Understanding the World (UW) and Expressive Arts and Design (EAD), to consider in thinking about how your curriculum meets children's needs.

Table 6.3 Skills: UW and EAD

UW	Where and when?	EAD	Where and when?
Developing curiosity and interest in own story and own family		Experimenting with blocks, colours and marks	
Learning about differences and similarities between self and others		Exploring colour and finding ways that colours can be changed; finding out about texture	
Becoming interested in other people and what they do as an occupation		Representing objects with lines to enclose a space	
Recalling and talking about own significant life experiences and those connected to friends and family		Creating sounds by banging, shaking, tapping or blowing; finding ways of changing sounds	
Joining in customs and routines of own family and with enthusiasm and finding out about other people's customs and traditions		Enjoying songs and rhymes and learning some songs and dances	
Noticing features of the place they live in or the natural world		Using construction materials; building to make enclosures	
Talking about things they have observed such as plants, animals, natural objects		Using tools and techniques to shape, assemble and join materials	
Noticing and talking about living things and the environment and the way things change over time		Pretending to do or be something or someone; pretending one thing stands for another, e.g. a block is a phone	

UW	Where and when?	EAD	Where and when?
Finding out about how to operate simple equipment or technological toys		Developing own ideas to create responses to experiences	
Selecting and using technology for particular purposes and beginning to discuss its uses		Representing own ideas in D&T, art, music, dance, role play and stories	

There are no prizes for noting how many resources are involved in providing for children to develop their understanding of the world and their creativity so clearly it is important that children have access to a wide range of resources and experiences, including those which inspire them to notice and talk about the place they live in, and all of the other things that share their habitat such as plants, animals and things in the living world like conkers, rocks, stones, twigs, animal prints, and so on. The way children respond to the world is through the 'hundred' languages referred to by Malaguzzi with reference to his work in Reggio Emilia. How we help children give voice to those languages is through helping them to decide how they will respond to what they see, touch, smell, hear or feel. This may be through movement, art, storytelling, drawing, writing, making, imagining or exploring and experimenting with a range of materials – and it is different for every child. Finally, consider what should be provided in order to support children to develop the skills required for the remaining specific areas of literacy and mathematics. Reading and Writing are shown below first for your consideration:

Table 6.4 Skills: Reading and Writing

Reading	Where and when	Writing	Where and when
Developing an interest in books		Developing interest in words, pictures and signs	
Enjoying rhymes, stories, poems and songs		Making marks to which they attribute meaning	
Joining in with refrains		Segmenting sounds heard into separate parts	
Learning about what pictures represent		Learning which sounds are represented by different graphemes	
Learning about words and writing		Blending sounds to create real and made up words	

Reading	Where and when	Writing	Where and when
Attending to and distinguishing different sounds		Distinguishing between pictures and writing	
Distinguishing sounds in words; recognising words of significance		Beginning to write using clearly identifiable letters	
Beginning to read some words using phonics		Writing own name or labels or captions	
Reading some common irregular words		Writing sentences using phonic knowledge	
		Reading own writing	

From the above, it is plain to see that every EYFS unit should have an abundance of books (not all out at the same time or only in one area – books should be everywhere) as well as opportunities for mark making, drawing and writing. The presence of books and mark-making materials in the environment gives messages about the importance of reading, mark making and writing in our society, yet without observing them in use children may show little interest in such activities. Therefore, it is essential that stories are shared regularly with children and that they learn to care for books and to understand their purpose. The same holds true for mark making and writing: unless children see the purpose and relevance of written communication their interest in mark making may be short-lived.

Ideally, in the EYFS, young children should learn to enjoy books, stories, songs and rhymes for the pleasure these bring as well as engage in mark making using many different media and tools. Adding props, puppets and other enhancements to a book basket dedicated to a story such as *Giraffes Can't Dance* by Giles Andreae and Guy Parker-Rees will extend children's engagement with the narrative whilst also helping them to understand the vocabulary as well as some of the key scenes. Providing prompts such as those described will encourage children to think about different characters and different parts of the story and lay the foundations for children to retell their favourite parts of the story, which, in time, will support them to retell whole stories and to create their own stories. Similarly, when a child sees other children or adults mark making they begin to learn about ways of communicating their ideas and this encourages them to develop their own skills as mark makers, picture makers and writers. It should be noted that the way reading and writing are taught in schools is not prescribed in the EYFS (at time of publication) although Ofsted has recently reported on issues with the teaching of writing. However, bear in mind this publication is not strictly policy (though it may become so in future).

The final, though, by no means least important, of the specific areas to reflect on is mathematical development shown in Table 6.5.

Table 6.5 Skills: Numbers and Space, shape and measures

Numbers	Where and when	Shape, space and measures	Where and when
Singing and saying numbers		Recognising differences in size	
Selecting numbers of objects		Fitting shapes into spaces or pieces into a jigsaw	
Counting small number of objects		Noticing shapes and patterns; recognising, creating and describing patterns	
Knowing when there are 'a lot' or 'a few' items in a set		Categorising objects in relation to shape or size and using the language of size	
Using number names in play and reciting numbers in order to ten		Talking about the shapes of everyday objects	
Representing numbers, using marks or fingers or pictures		Selecting and naming common shapes	
Comparing numbers and separating sets of objects in different ways, e.g. 2 and 2		Understanding the pattern of the day	
Recognising numerals and finding correct number of items to match the numeral; finding more or less		Understanding 'time' words, such as before, later or soon	
Counting to 20, ordering them and saying which is one more or less than a given number		Talking about size, weight, capacity, position, distance, time and money to compare quantities, and objects to solve problems.	
Solving problems including doubling, halving and sharing		Using mathematical language	

Many children arrive at school or nursery recognising some numbers and many more arrive able to say some numbers in order (by rote). That is, they can often say the numbers from one to five, ten, or twenty. A common misunderstanding when children are able to do this is that this constitutes counting and/or one-to-one recognition. However, this is not necessarily the case because recognition of a numeral is merely one aspect of the child 'getting' number. The ability to know what the numeral represents is a different aspect, as is finding the correct number of items each numeral represents. It is important that adults in school and parents at home understand how essential it is that young children should develop an understanding of concepts such as the 'threeness' of three or the 'fourness' of four as a foundation for mathematics, because gaining an understanding of numbers to ten will form the basis of later mathematical understanding.

The place of Shape, space and measures (SSM) in the curriculum for the youngest children is also important to future mathematicians, architects, engineers, medics and many other skilled workers because as much as children develop knowledge about these things, they also develop beliefs about their own abilities very early and can be turned 'on' or 'off' such subjects depending on whether they feel they are successful or unsuccessful at them. Indeed, research shows that '*the unique contribution of positive attitude(s) to maths achievement is as large as the contribution of IQ*' (Chen et al., 2017).

A review of SSM shows that this is as much about the language of mathematics as it is about knowledge of shapes, space and measures. Therefore, provision in the EYFS should reflect this and teaching should be based around children's interests as they engage in play in, for example, a veterinary surgery where they can weigh out a supply of food for a dog or estimate which box will best fit a sick animal.

Gather resources to support children's interests

Making your environment 'special'

How you make your environment special will reflect your own strengths and the interests of the children at different times of the year. In winter it may be a wonderland of snow scenes, lights and mysterious packages and in spring it may be centred on growing as many things as possible and reflective of visits to a farm. Whatever it is like it should be a special place where staff and children can engage with a variety of resources both open ended and those which have a predictable outcome such as puzzles and games.

Making your environment feel like a 'special place'

Key takeaway

It may be helpful to think about your EYFS space like a retail store manager – who knows which lines sell and are worth space on the shop floor – and to consider why (as a manager of the learning environment) you give space to some things over others. It is also a good plan to find your unique selling point – the thing that distinguishes your provision from others and makes your environment 'special'.

Whatever you decide upon try to focus on developing it to the best of your ability (in terms of the resources you can afford/beg/borrow or steal). An environment that hooks children in is full of surprises such as a letter arriving in the home corner, a shiny tin appearing in the small world area or a trail of fairy dust leading to a potion recipe. Any of these things, carefully planned, can spark children's interest so that they respond in all manner of ways.

An issue connected to this is when children 'transport' materials from one place to another. This sometimes can be a source of frustration as adults try to keep track of resources they have painstakingly sorted out, only to find them in a heap elsewhere, requisitioned by an enthusiastic four-year-old for a purpose the adult couldn't even guess at. Keeping the environment and resources in a good state is everybody's responsibility so at the end of the day, unless the appropriated items are fundamental to say a building, then they should be returned to where they normally 'live' so that they can be found on the next occasion that somebody requires them. A colleague I have worked with closely taught me that every early years teacher should adopt the following mantra about the use of resources: 'Choose, Use and Return'! It takes some time to establish this but it certainly works so perhaps if you don't use it currently you might want to try it. The important thing is that every child and adult should know the place of each resource so that when something is needed everybody knows where to find it.

Sources

Ofsted school inspection handbook August 2018

- 'Teaching in the early years … takes account of the equipment adults provide and the attention given to the physical environment, as well as the structure and routines of the day that establish expectations. Integral to teaching is how practitioners assess what children know, understand and can do, as well as taking account of their interests and dispositions to learn (characteristics of effective learning), and how practitioners use this information to plan children's next steps in learning and monitor their progress.' (Page 35, footnote 63)

- 'Inspectors will consider:

  how well teaching nurtures, engages and motivates children and promotes their sense of achievement and commitment to learning the breadth of the curriculum and how well it is based on accurate assessment of children's learning and development, so that activities and experiences meet their needs children's enjoyment of learning, including their participation and willingness to make choices and decisions, and the extent to which children are active and inquisitive learners who are creative and think critically.' (Pages 58–59)

Statutory framework for the early years foundation stage: Setting the standards for learning, development and care for children from birth to five (2017)

- 'Children learn and develop well in **enabling environments**, in which their experiences respond to their individual needs and there is a strong partnership between practitioners and parents and/or carers.' (Page 6)

7 Continuous provision: Creating challenges for learning

Key Points

- Overcome the biggest challenge by ensuring that the 'hooks', 'provocations' or 'challenges' you add to continuous provision are varied and inviting – otherwise children and adults will learn to ignore them

- Model the approaches and attitudes you want to inspire in children so they are willing to 'have a go' (and can cope with not getting it right first time) after trying various challenges

- When you want children to consolidate particular aspects of learning, find new ways to reach the same outcomes so that they enjoy learning through play

- Consult the children to find ways to expand challenges in particular areas of provision

Varied and inviting 'challenges'

Teachers often tell me they have great difficulty in setting up exciting, interesting challenges in the continuous provision and since every area of the environment has to support play and learning (in the way a member of staff would do), it's important to get this area right.

The first challenge is often ensuring that what is added to continuous provision, in the way of enhancements, is both intriguing and novel. This may vary depending on children's interests – some may be 'hooked' at the first sight of a fluffy toy cat and a cat basket or by a bowl of soapy water, pegs and a washing line, whilst others may be thrilled to find head and wrist bands alongside cloaks so that they can explore taking on superhuman powers. Almost anything new we provide is bound to be a hit if it captures children's imaginations or if it is considered by them to be worthy of further exploration.

However, novelty doesn't last so we need to be mindful of this and not expect the same reaction a week, or even a few days later, when something new has lost its initial appeal. For example, a range of spy glasses, telescopes and binoculars may provoke a great deal of interest initially but unless we help children to see the potential of these items they may lie unused alongside more everyday items. In a sense this is one value of identifying challenges because they can give children clues as to how to engage with resources with which they are not familiar. By adding challenges, we can not only hook children in but we can often engage them fully, too.

Perhaps the most daunting aspect of creating challenges in continuous provision is that adults are sometimes a little like long-distance runners who are over-ambitious at the outset and then find that their energy is spent before they can complete the race. Hence, the feeling expressed to me by so many teachers is that setting challenges is something that they have tried but which became too unwieldy and was therefore abandoned.

The value of setting challenges very much depends on what is on offer – some challenges may be very worthwhile whilst others may be a complete waste of time and effort. It's important to be clear that in addition to giving children ideas for how to use resources, the purpose of providing any challenge is to motivate and engage children in some of the following ways (though this is not an exhaustive list):

- **Finding out**: exploring and playing with items and materials to understand more about them

- **Making guesses**: hypothesising about what might happen if something is done, changed, added or taken away (the possibilities are endless)

- **Problem-solving by using a range of strategies**: recognising that different strategies may succeed or fail (skills that many adults find difficult)

- **Reviewing their actions**: evaluating how something was done, whether it worked or not and how it might be improved.

Managing challenges

To be successful, challenges need to be fresh and tempting – rather than well-used or predictable, otherwise everybody, including adults, loses interest in them and they become like wallpaper that people have stopped seeing. If you want to offer 'hooks' for children's learning, starting small is a good way to begin because there is a fair chance that you will be able to keep up the pace if you do this. If, initially, you introduce one challenge you will be able to monitor this to identify whether what you have offered is at the right level and is interesting for all of the children. If this challenge proves exciting and interesting then you can develop a plan to cover more areas or to differentiate some challenges so that different groups of children can enjoy reaching a satisfying outcome for their efforts. It may be useful to begin by either:

a) thinking about the areas where play is less well-developed, perhaps in a home corner, a water tray or the sand tray

or

b) thinking about areas of learning for which you have fewer observations because of some limitation in your provision or practice. For example, you might find you have a dearth of meaningful observations for '*Health and self-care: children know the import-ance for good health of physical exercise…*' (DfE, 2017:11), suggesting your provision is either not set up to capture this aspect accurately or that it has been overlooked for some reason – perhaps when the tablet wasn't charged!

So, in order to manage challenges, here are some guidelines:

- Start small, beginning by consulting with the children. They may say they want a net so that they can play basketball and you could then obtain one.

- Once you have identified a possible focus discuss with the children how the challenge will work. Will they need a timer or will they have five turns at getting the ball in the net before another child can have a turn?

- Once this is established you might want to create a self-registration process so all interested children will know when they can have their turn.

- And finally, you may want to make the challenge easier or more difficult for the younger/older, smaller/bigger, less/more mature children. Perhaps expect bigger children to stand near one line and smaller children closer to the net to take their 'shots'.

Once you decide to extend learning possibilities for children you may find that this approach becomes a significant part of your provision because children will enjoy the independence and autonomy which is often lacking in more formal learning environments where a child's choices may be restricted and opportunities for exploring and finding out are fewer.

Model the approaches and attitudes you want to inspire

If you choose to create challenges, it will be important to ensure that you model the approaches and attitudes you want to see. If you want to encourage children to a challenge in the home corner identify what sorts of things will interest them – it may be that adding a siphon of water to the kitchen supplies will be a game changer with the challenge of using it to fill the cups to a marked line when they are playing, spilling as little as possible. Dependent on what you want children to achieve from challenges, it will be important to identify the potential learning from the challenges as well as to plan how you will communicate what they involve. Will they, for example, be something that you talk about to a group of children, will you tell the whole class or will they be something that children can discover more about when they press a talking postcard? No method is wholly reliable so you may wish to work with a small group who become 'challenge champions' for a morning until others are as expert as they are at completing the task.

Challenges are also about learning that not every attempt will be a success and that they should persist by using trial and error. Try to ensure that whatever you offer is open ended and largely failure-proof so that children can cope with not getting it right first time. In this way you can teach the importance of 'having a go' at something and children can begin to understand that learning is not always about getting the 'right answer' and that there is more than one way of doing things.

The idea that learning is either right or wrong is often the reason that children experience feelings of failure very early on in their school lives so it is really important that they see the teacher, TA and any other helpers experiencing both positive and negative outcomes for things they try to do. Activities that support skill development can be great fun at the same time as acting as a useful reminder that everybody succeeds and fails from time to time. For example, I have lost count of the number of times I have painstakingly stood a series of dominoes on end to show a child how to do a domino run then knocked one down before I had finished setting up the run – the end result is always that the children delightedly try to do better than me and usually succeed.

Playing games like Pick-Up Sticks or Jenga™ illustrate for children that even when the adults are taking care, like children, they can very easily destabilise the pieces, so setting up challenges like this can work to support things like manual dexterity, concentration and resilience. Games such as Ludo™ or 'The House That Jack Built™', based on throwing a coloured dice to collect pieces of a house comprising of windows, garage doors, front door, roof and chimneys are also good because of the 'chance' aspect so that children learn that skill is not the only thing that counts in completing some challenges.

Whilst for more able children, challenges like 'spot the difference' and playing games such as Guess Who™ are excellent at encouraging them to compare things and to make deductions. However, few schools are able to devote the time needed to encouraging children to play games though if you have the good fortune to have a student or other helper this would be a wonderful use of their time. Failing this additional support, open-ended challenges are a great idea to encourage exploration. Table 7.2 at the end of the chapter has 50 open-ended challenges you might want to think about. Identify for yourself the possible learning from each challenge and whether any might be useful, if differentiated or modified, to suit the needs of the children in your school.

Learning through play

There may be some challenges that are about achievement of a particular skill, for example, certain handwriting skills being encouraged after all other necessary physical skills are established. Challenges in nursery might have focused on the direction of lines, creating for example, a cage for a lion by painting or making marks in shaving foam from top to bottom to create lots of vertical lines, precursors of formation of letters such as 'l' and 'i', etc. Whilst in Reception, it may be that what is called for is the formation of anti-clockwise shapes. I once saw a teacher encouraging a child to do this by inviting them to draw the feathers for a swan's wing. The child persevered lengthily to make the movements to create a lot of feathers for the wings, all looking remarkably like 'c's.

> ## Key takeaway
>
> The important thing is to make learning fun and for children to feel successful in their learning. Indeed, by modelling a 'growth mindset' we teach children some of the most important personal skills – that is, to be persistent and to believe they can improve their skills by practising. Skills such as skipping, hopping, throwing and catching a ball are learned in this way as are number bonds, dance moves and mixing and blending paint colours.

Spontaneity and freedom are words often used to describe children's time in the EYFS, when children should be encouraged to explore the learning environment and to make their own choices. Yet many Reception classes in schools are bound by almost impossible timetables, covering everything from attendance at assemblies to phonics, guided reading, guided writing, maths sessions, RE, music, PE and so on, leaving a minimum amount of time for assimilation of new knowledge, reflection on learning and consolidation. Effective continuous provision can reduce the need for this fragmented approach by offering children alternative ways of learning and giving teachers the chance to work with them in depth on a particular area of interest.

Consult the children

Think about a child with an encyclopaedic knowledge of animals who is completely and utterly focused on them, and imagine the joy they feel at being able to return to this subject again and again. Some children are preoccupied with such a singular interest for a long period, whilst others have more fleeting interests inspired by lived experiences such as: going on a woodland trail, finding bugs, spotting aeroplanes, pretending to be pirates, riding ponies, becoming superheroes, throwing birthday parties, splashing in puddles, dressing up, going shopping – the list is endless. Other children may spend a great length of time engaged in exploring different aspects of unicorns, whilst others might dip in and out of interests because of a particular need, e.g. a need to be moving all the time, such as the boy who said to me recently, 'I need to do this to think' as he walked round and round the room. These pursuits, whether short or long, reveal 'schema' or patterns of behaviour that knowledgeable adults endeavour to support through talking to children and identifying with them where they want go in their enquiry or what they want to do next.

Consulting children can be achieved informally through talking to them, following their lead and taking on board their suggestions. Often, they may want to go back to an 'interest' that has run its course in the class but which for some reason appeals to them in the present. This might be space travel or planting and growing vegetables, or it might be a story or setting up a show weeks after the parents' assembly when they acted the part of a sheep in the class play. Allowing for these interests may help children to come to an understanding of an important event, concept or idea which they may not be able to express but which they feel an urge to explore. This will, in time, bring new understandings and will enable them to move on in their learning.

Consider the ways of consulting with children in Table 7.1, identifying which of the statements in the three middle columns best describe your current approach.

When you have completed this evaluation, you may want to think about what you could note down in the fourth column so that what is on offer in your school is a true reflection of children's interests, pre-occupations and needs.

Table 7.1 Consulting children

How we consult with children	Established	Developing	On my radar	Something I should consider
Share observations with them and talk to them about what they enjoyed and would like to do next				
Seek feedback from parents about what aspects of learning were enjoyed by their child				
Ask children to give a thumbs up or down to things, e.g. a visit to the zoo or a farm				

How we consult with children	Established	Developing	On my radar	Something I should consider
Ask for children's ideas about changing something such as. an area of provision and act on what they say				
Ask pairs of children to discuss and give feedback about experiences or activities we propose but are willing to modify or change in some way				
Encourage children to identify areas of interest they would like to explore further or revisit				
Identify when, or if, children want to retain something ephemeral such as a model they have made that they may want to return to at another time				
Enable them to be honest about the things they enjoy and those they find hard				
Challenge stereotypes by encouraging boys and girls to accept others' choices and to feel OK about doing so				
Offer role models to emphasise non-stereotypical activities or experiences such as inviting in a male nurse, a female fire officer or a male who cooks or cares for children				

If you are like one of the many teachers who have not yet got around to embracing the challenges of ensuring that continuous provision really reels children in, then you might want to begin by planning your approach now. If one challenge works, try developing another challenge in the same way, remembering to ensure that everything is properly prepared so that children don't end up competing for resources or discover the whole challenge has been dismantled, moved or trashed.

Finally, the purpose of a challenge is not simply to encourage children to do something they can already do, rather it is to encourage them to try and to explore and find new ways of doing things – at the same time as it is for teaching to focus on encouraging them to be divergent thinkers. Once you decide to extend learning possibilities for children you may find that this approach becomes a significant part of your provision because children will enjoy the independence and autonomy which is often lacking in more formal learning environments where their choices may be restricted and opportunities for exploring and finding out are few and far between.

Children are invited to make their own game – effective continuous provision can provide children with alternative ways of learning

Table 7.2 Fifty challenges

Challenge	Resources	Purpose/Potential Learning	Differentiation
1. Make a bed for baby bear.	Bears, boxes, material		
2. Can you help Batman get down from the tree?	Batman, tree, nets, material		
3. Bobo the monkey wants a swing.	Monkey toy, string, sticky tape, twigs, material		
4. How many times can you fill the cup from the milk carton?	½ litre milk carton, (transparent) small cup, additional container		

Challenge	Resources	Purpose/Potential Learning	Differentiation
5. Tell the story of *Jack and the Beanstalk* with the props.	Tuff tray, wooden or soft characters/puppets of Jack, the giant, Jack's mother, beanstalk, hen, gold, etc.		
6. Teach Gerald the Giraffe a dance.	Percussion instruments, giraffe, story of *Giraffes Can't Dance* by Giles Andreae and Guy Parker-Rees		
7. Stack the monkeys to see how many you can balance.	Stacking monkeys		
8. Build a bridge so the Billy Goats Gruff can cross into the field.	Tuff tray, ½ fake grass, ½ plain blocks, three goats, troll		

Challenge	Resources	Purpose/Potential Learning	Differentiation
9. Hide three soft toys. Put a cross on the map to show where you hid them.	Map of classroom (discussed previously), pencil or felt pen, three soft toys, finder (another child)		
10. Guess how many balls will fit in the box. Try it and see if you were right.	Shoe box, selection of water bomb balls		
11. Use the shells and stones to make a pattern in the sand.	Shells of different types, stones, sand, tray large enough to leave room for a pattern		
12. How many stones will make the water come over the top of the bucket?	Small bucket filled with water, pile of small pebbles, white board and marker, tray for bucket		

Challenge	Resources	Purpose/Potential Learning	Differentiation
13. Fix the yellow Duplo® pieces together – do they reach the top of the door?	Yellow Duplo®, space		
14. Make a green mixture for a witch's spell.	Powder paint: yellow, blue, black, water, cornflour, glitter		
15. Put the shoes on the spider. How many pairs did you use?	Boxes of old, clean shoes, picture of a spider, space for child to tally pairs required		
16. Can you label the parts of the fish?	Picture of a class goldfish with magnetic labels to place around it		

Challenge	Resources	Purpose/Potential Learning	Differentiation
17. How many pennies can you fit in the box?	Box, one pence pieces		
18. Can you make pies for four people and a dog?	Mud, cake trays or cupcake cases		
19. Can you make a home for a lost hedgehog?	Hedgehogs, straws, saucers, material		
20. Draw some lines with the ruler to make a road for a car.	Large ruler, big pieces of paper, toy cars, thick felt pens		

Challenge	Resources	Purpose/Potential Learning	Differentiation
21. Can you make some words like: tap, mat, dump, tent?	Magnetic letters, magnetic board		
22. Can you make a banana sandwich?	Bananas, bread, butter or spread, plates, knives		
23. Can you find some ways to make ten?	Large piece of paper, Numicon™, counters, felt pens		
24. Find five things that are bigger than your shoe.	Pumps, boxes for collecting items		

Challenge	Resources	Purpose/Potential Learning	Differentiation
25. Find ten things that are smaller than your shoe.	Pumps, boxes for collecting items		
26. Use the tweezers to fill the box with pompoms.	Tweezers, pompoms, boxes		
27. Put the ponies in the right stables.	Ponies, ribbons round each to match colour of stables		
28. Paint the paper all over. Wait for it to dry. Peel off the tape.	Paper with sticky tape in random places – to create resistance to paint		

Challenge	Resources	Purpose/Potential Learning	Differentiation
29. Make a picture in the frame.	Frame, found items such as leaves, twigs, beads, dried flowers, nut shells, string, etc.		
30. Make a spider's web.	Large plastic needles, wool, stiff cards with holes in		
31. Make your mark!	Table, paper fixed to table, range of mark makers such as glue, pastels, felt pens, crayons, powder paint		
32. Build a tower that is taller than you.	Blocks, space		

Challenge	Resources	Purpose/Potential Learning	Differentiation
33. Build a tower shorter than you.	Blocks, space		
34. Build a tower the same height as you.	Blocks, space		
35. Tell a story to the teddy.	Teddy bear, choice of books from basket		
36. Learn this poem and say it to the class.	Laminated typed sheets with short familiar poems		
37. Read a book to a friend.	Friend, book at correct reading level		

Challenge	Resources	Purpose/Potential Learning	Differentiation
38. Roll the jack five times. How many skittles can you knock down?	Skittles, jack, paper and pencil for tallying		
39. Get the dolls ready to go out to play.	Large dolls (boys and girls), realistic clothes including fleeces, bobby hats, etc.		
40. How many hops can you do in a minute?	Clipboard with child's name and dates for child to record on so as to compete against their previous best, felt pens		
41. Cut up the bananas and cucumber into slices for your table.	Bananas, cucumber, knife, plate, chopping board		

Challenge	Resources	Purpose/Potential Learning	Differentiation
42. Count the wrist bands. How many for shepherd's pie, cheese pie, fish pie?	Coloured wrist bands, pictures of different dinners, chalks and boards		
43. Build a Batmobile with crates.	Crates, space, driving wheels, material		
44. Make a den for two children.	Material, sticks, pegs, cushions		
45. Put the story cards in the right order. Put a hoop over the picture you like best.	Story cards with main events from stories such as *What the Ladybird Heard* by Julia Donaldson and Lydia Monks, *The Little Red Hen*, etc., hoop		

Challenge	Resources	Purpose/Potential Learning	Differentiation
46. Guess who is tallest: elephant, rhino or hippo?	Three animals with heads poking out of box, card with animal pictures above each of the three columns, ticks on cards with self-fasteners to stick on chosen column		
47. Wrap a parcel with paper and sticky tape.	Several parcels, wrapping paper, brown paper, sticky tape, scissors		
48. The animals have got into the wrong pens. Can you sort them out?	Small world farm animals, pens or enclosures, labels with animal species, e.g. pigs		
49. How many stones/beads in the bottle?	Sealed jar containing different sized stones or beads, clipboard, paper with list of children's names, columns for children to write in their guesses, pencil		

Challenge	Resources	Purpose/Potential Learning	Differentiation
50. Find five things inside the home corner that start with 'w'. Write a list of them.	Sufficient items to make this doable, e.g. whisk, window, washing machine, wellies, washing up liquid, plus paper, pencils, felt pens		

Sources

Ofsted school inspection handbook August 2018

'Teaching… takes account of the equipment adults provide and the attention given to the physical environment, as well as the structure and routines of the day that establish expectations. **Integral to teaching is** how practitioners assess what children know, understand and can do, as well as **taking account of their interests and dispositions to learn (characteristics of effective learning), and how practitioners use this information to plan children's next steps in learning** and monitor their progress.' (Page 58)

Teachers' standards 2013

'A teacher must:

- set high expectations which inspire, motivate and challenge pupils
- set goals that stretch and challenge pupils of all backgrounds, abilities and dispositions
- demonstrate consistently the positive attitudes, values and behaviour which are expected of pupils.' (Page 7)

8 Widening opportunities: Outdoor learning

Key Points

- Consult parents and children to find out what children like to do outdoors
- Plan for outdoor learning with the same rigour as for indoor learning
- Audit your outdoor provision every half term so that it continues to interest children; act as a role model so that children understand the potential of different areas of the outdoor learning environment
- Optimise opportunities for play and learning outside so that different learning styles are accommodated and the requirements of the EYFS are met

Whilst most teachers are very confident about the environment for learning inside school, many teachers say they know their outdoor learning environment is a work in progress – something they have not quite got around to *yet*. Often their reason for this is uncertainty about justifying play outdoors – and this is not surprising since many headteachers seem concerned that Ofsted inspections focus on the learning and progress that is demonstrated indoors, rather than on the quality of play and learning seen outside. Whether this is true or not is debatable though, according to many teachers, inspectors rarely seem to spend much time outdoors on visits to EYFS. So, the focus of this chapter is to challenge your thinking about this important area and to help you get the best from your outdoor learning environment.

On a bright day in spring when there is only a light breeze, it's easy to offer interesting and exciting activities outdoors but on wintry days when the weather is dark and grey, the ground is waterlogged and the wind is biting, it can seem that these things are an impossibility. However, it is worth remembering that the EYFS states:

'Providers must provide access to an outdoor play area or, if that is not possible, ensure that outdoor activities are planned and taken on a daily basis (unless circumstances make this inappropriate, for example unsafe weather conditions)' (DfE, 2017:30).

So, whatever the weather, schools should ensure that outdoor activities are available and, in order to do this successfully, it is well worth investing in suitable clothing for both children and adults alike. Once this has been done then it is much more likely that outdoor learning will take place and be enjoyable for everybody concerned!

Consulting parents and children

Some children don't have many opportunities for being out in a big space and so many just enjoy experiencing the freedom this brings, feeling the wind in their hair and the pleasure of being free to run around and climb and jump as much as they want to. This is a perfectly valid thing for them to do and once they realise that this is available every day they will eventually turn to doing other things such as pouring water through bendy pipes, digging a raised bed or making a dyke in a water-filled culvert. An obvious way of finding out what children like to do outdoors is inviting their parents to share the things their children do at weekends, some of which will be outside activities. You may place a pile of leaf shapes in a basket for parents to write on and hang on a tree or invite parents to text you about the outdoor activities their children enjoy, such as using a hose to wash flagstones, collecting leaves, making a den and so on.

When we consult children about what they like to do outdoors it might be difficult for them to think beyond what they played with that day or the day before, so it's worth helping them to consider this by showing them photos of possible activities such as:

- Mark making with snow/hail/sand/paint/felt pens/chalks/rice/coffee granules/shaving foam/chocolate sauce
- Digging in sand/soil using a range of tools such as scoops, spades, plant pots
- Transporting materials such as leaves, blocks, sand, soil, pebbles, twigs
- Climbing/balancing/hopping/running/riding on wheeled toys
- Making transient art using natural materials such as grasses/flower heads/twigs/fir cones/acorns/leaves
- Making music with beaters/pipes/water-filled bottles/found items
- Playing characters from stories, with props, to create scenarios from their favourite stories or rhymes
- Tending to plants or living things by preparing food; feeding the school's pets such as rabbits or chickens
- Enjoying books in a cosy tent or natural structure
- Observing, imagining, talking in dens or hideaways
- Gathering things from the garden to share or to use in potions
- Following a treasure trail with visual or sensory clues
- Exploring with binoculars, magnifiers and cameras
- Rescuing model dinosaurs from a pit and making them a new home out of twigs and stones
- Putting on a show and issuing tickets with seat numbers

- Riding wheeled toys and setting up a washing/repair point

- Bathing dolls and washing their clothes

- Finding ways to melt ice in a bucket to extract a frozen figure such as Superman

- Building a structure with wooden blocks

- Mixing powder paints in a large tray to see what happens when water is added to dry paint

- Digging and planting or weeding a grow bag, tub or bed

- Playing with bats and balls or throwing bean bags

- Making a tower for a beanstalk to grow up

- Finding a fast way for a Jack figure to escape from the giant.

The possible list is endless and is only intended as an example of a tasting platter that might be developed, based on children's current interests, the weather and the season. It might also be possible to develop photobooks for each season so that what is depicted is available. There's little point in putting out small buckets of water to freeze Superman in ice overnight in the summer, whereas on some winter nights that's perfectly possible!

Whatever resources and equipment are available and whatever children choose to do, the most important resource of all is adult input – whether that is in the form of introducing new ideas or enhancements, being a partner in the play or fostering affirming relationships. The role of the skilled adult is varied. They may simply station themselves alongside a child in order to give them the confidence to persist in their chosen activity, or act as a resource provider, introduce new ideas, provide a commentary on what the child is doing or join in the play – following the child's agenda. I recently did this in a nursery where a shy child was carefully having a go at mixing white gloop in a tuff tray, using a chopstick. Picking up another chopstick I knelt beside him, mirroring his actions with the gloop. As we continued our explorations of the gloop, we were joined by four more children who each tried different mark-making implements.

This led to discussions about how the gloop could be moved like a solid at the edges of the tray yet was fluid enough to drip back into the tray when lifted on a spoon. As these discussions continued one child was struck by the similarity between the white gloop and snow and this acted as a prompt for the others to think about Christmas. Soon, one after another, they chimed in to tell me that at Christmas we have 'pudding' and 'turkey' and 'presents' and 'sparkly shoes'. This animated conversation led on to discussions about the shoes one of the girls was wearing that day and the fact that her daddy had bought them for her.

Supporting children to remain engaged in an activity such as this, which contributes to gross motor development and to take turns at speaking and listening, is an important consideration in terms of PSED as well as language development, and of course, writing. Using what is known about children's interests then allows practitioners to reflect these in the resources and activities that are available in the outdoor area so that the children can pursue whatever line of enquiry they'd like to when they are in this environment again.

The stage is set to create a space where dinosaurs might be brought to life

Rigour in planning for outdoor learning

Consider which of the activities in Table 8.1 are routinely planned for and taught in the outdoor and indoor areas. Next to the area of teaching and learning in the table, make a note of why each is planned to take place in the different environments. Then in the next column identify if adults are informed of children's next steps by adding 'Yes' or 'No' to that column. Finally, consider which activities are done by teachers (TEs) and which by teaching assistants (TAs).

When you have completed the table, analyse your findings to see if what you plan to teach outdoors is given equal importance as to what is planned for indoors. Then consider and discuss the balance of teaching between teachers and teaching assistants and how adults are made aware of the 'Next Steps' in children's learning. You should also consider which areas of learning are more rigorously or more loosely planned, e.g. how detailed is planning for language development compared with what is planned for phonics?

Table 8.1 Planning for teaching in and out of doors

WHAT IS TAUGHT:	INDOORS	Next Steps	TAs/TEs?	OUTDOORS	Next Steps	TAs/TEs?
PD: Fine motor development						
PD: Gross motor development						
Speaking and listening						
Understanding and social interaction, e.g. turn-taking in conversation						
Phonics						
Guided reading						

WHAT IS TAUGHT:	INDOORS	Next Steps	TAs/TEs?	OUTDOORS	Next Steps	TAs/TEs?
Guided writing						
Individual reads						
Writing: Composition						
Handwriting						
Maths						
PSED: Circle time						
Story						

WHAT IS TAUGHT:	INDOORS	Next Steps	TAs/TEs?	OUTDOORS	Next Steps	TAs/TEs?
UW: The World						
RE						
EAD: Music						
EAD: Singing						
EAD: Making/Craft						

If everything is balanced well, that's excellent; you are obviously not placing greater value on one area over another. However, you are also quite unusual because many EYFS leaders in schools often tell me that although they are committed to outdoor learning they do not plan for learning in the outdoor environment with as much rigour as they provide inside the classrooms. This can then lead children and adults to the view that 'real learning' takes place inside the school rather than outside, which can lead to the idea that the play that takes place out of doors is simply an opportunity for well-earned movement when children have done a lot of sitting. Clearly, this view of teaching and learning is inaccurate.

Another issue that often emerges when schools are still working to get outdoor learning 'right' is that whilst the resources and equipment may be available, out of doors the teaching and learning aren't focused sufficiently. When this happens, opportunities for effective teaching and learning can be lost. Picture a scenario I witnessed in a school, where a substantial area had been given over to construction and a large group of children were enthusiastically moving blocks from place to place. In spite of all their activity, the adult, whose role was to teach all the children, spent time with just one child helping them to select pairs of shapes from big cards in a shape den. Clearly, getting the balance right can be difficult, which can mean that although many potential learning situations occur these are not always fully exploited. For this reason, it is crucial that everybody who is working with the children knows their learning needs and is focused on supporting them to make the next steps in their learning. The best way to do this is to ensure that all children are observed regularly over a short period so that rather than gathering several observations of a child demonstrating the same skills, only significant steps are captured, such as when a child calculates that if three and two make five then two and three must also make the same amount.

Auditing your outdoor provision

Taking a hard look at your outdoor area can sometimes be painful particularly between seasons when the weather may have been unremittingly wet and time short. I have been invited to several schools, particularly in early spring when staff are wanting to make a fresh start, knowing that what they have been offering hasn't always come up to scratch in terms of engaging children in deep level learning. One thing we do is get out into the outdoor area with the proforma in Table 8.2. This allows us to make notes about what we have seen so that when we return inside we have tangible pieces of information.

Table 8.2 Auditing Outdoor Provision (1)

Observe children outside: Note what they are doing; what they are using and where they spend time	Ask the children about what they like to do outside:
Identify what opportunities are available for play and learning:	Ask the children what could be changed or made better outside:

Whilst we walk around doing our research we take photos of the different resources and areas of provision. What often emerges is that things have become 'invisible' such as an upturned table lying in the covered area; an old truck that has lost its wheels or a derelict garden that once produced strawberries and other food which now lies neglected. Only when we look at the photos do these things become visible. At this point we sometimes consider the following questions:

Table 8.3 Auditing Outdoor Provision (2)

Current set up: What is the outdoor area like? What play, learning and teaching are taking place?	What works? Consider opportunities for independent activity, teaching opportunities, the environment and resources
What is limiting or could be developed?	Any ideas or solutions to improve the current offer?

Having this discussion usually leads on to the next phase of the visit where we discuss the vision and values that underpin approaches to teaching and learning outdoors. At this point I am often met by silence because although this is something that is often implicit in the school's provision it's not always shared or fully understood by everybody concerned, including parents and the headteacher. When faced with this realisation (that they had no written vision or values about outdoor learning) a group of schools I worked with decided to explore a range of published guidelines to develop their shared vision focusing on publications such as 'Outdoor Learning' (Leicestershire County Council) which states:

> 'All children have the right to experience and enjoy the essential and special nature of being outdoors. Young children thrive and their minds and bodies develop best when they have free access to stimulating outdoor environments for learning through play and real experiences. Knowledgeable and enthusiastic adults are crucial to unlocking the potential of outdoors' (Leicestershire County Council:4).

The outcome from their reflections was their own vision, which they have kindly allowed me to reproduce here:

> 'As stated in the EYFS, children are entitled to outdoor opportunities for play and learning on a daily basis. Children thrive in the special nature of the outdoor environment through having opportunities to explore, develop their physical skills, and feed their imaginations. The outdoors can provide a range of different experiences from indoors, with the freedom for large scale activities. The enthusiasm, action, and interaction of adults with children, inspires, motivates and engages children in learning through play. Planning for play and learning outdoors is equally as important as planning for play and learning indoors' (Learning Network).

After considering different schools' vision and values we often then explore the provision further, auditing the space and resources. Many organisations such as Learning through Landscapes Cymru™ suggest the types of continuous provision resources (many of them sourced either free or very inexpensively) that schools might want to provide so that children can play and learn out of doors. Therefore, it is not my intention to suggest what resources are available in great detail; however, it is worth schools considering that for young children there needs to be a balance between predictable and novel items so that they are motivated and inspired to explore things newly each day. So, for example, in the role play area there may be a supermarket set up with a range of groceries and a till, together with shopping baskets and purses. Adding to this predictable offer you may enhance the provision by introducing a toy aisle in the weeks before Christmas or a gardening section in the spring. Introducing new items into an area can stimulate children's interests, taking their learning in a new direction. This might inspire the children to take photographs of the new items in store for a catalogue.

Using the evaluation schedule in Table 8.4 half termly (drawn from innumerable sources) has kick started discussions about the how and what of resources in the outdoor environment for schools I have worked with.

Table 8.4 Evaluation of Outdoor Provision

Excellent organisation of the outdoor space:	Established	Developing	On the radar	Something to consider
The area is risk assessed daily				
The area is attractive and inviting and is suitable for use in all weather				
The area is set out in zones which separate different types of activity such as bike riding and playing ball				
Resources are well-maintained and attractive and children can access them independently				
Resources include a range of items supporting play and learning across the prime and specific areas of the EYFS				
The outdoor space is treated as a learning environment where teaching is ongoing and adults are engaged with children in their play and learning				
Area for activities such as digging, planting and growing things				
Area for activities such as music making, acting and singing				
Area for activities such as mark making and sharing books				

Excellent organisation of the outdoor space:	Established	Developing	On the radar	Something to consider
Area for activities such as climbing, running and balancing				
Area for activities such as loading, filling and emptying a range of containers with different materials				
Area for activities such as filling and emptying containers with water with access to taps and guttering at different levels				
Area for activities such as imaginative play in for example a mud kitchen, den or hide				
Area for activities such as sitting quietly and reading or resting from time to time				
Area for activities such as investigation of wild life or observing birds feeding or building nests				
Area for activities such as den making or forest school				
Area for activities such as following trails, creating imaginative scenarios or riding a bike				

Once this has been discussed we consider the gap between what is available and what else the school might want to offer in the way of resources and areas where different things can take place. I am frequently told that bikes are a concern, with teachers aware of the importance of physical activity but conscious too of how extended bike use by children might be viewed if an inspector were to observe outdoor learning. Since the question of 'how long is too long?' is one that I have no simple answer to, I simply recall a school where after noting a boy had ridden a bike for long periods the inspector wrote in the report about the many opportunities to develop physical skills afforded to children in the setting. Ultimately, this decision is one which should be informed by the needs of individual children balanced against those of the whole group (and reached with a good helping of common sense)!

Helping children understand the potential of different areas outdoors

Children often only learn about expectations for using different resources and equipment either from what they are told or from their observations of what others do with them. Therefore, it's important to remember they need help to work out their purpose and what they can do with them. Modelling expectations is key to success because although open-ended play opportunities are planned there is often a purpose behind them which a child may not have understood, for example, perhaps a trolley is set out with materials such as sticky tape, masking tape and string to support children interested in playing at Amazon where they are receiving orders and wrapping and delivering parcels. This will work fine for the children who are in the 'know' but when a child, who isn't familiar with this scenario, comes along they may be excluded from the play because it is something they are not familiar with.

So, it's important to never assume that children will know what to do with certain resources and whilst we should recognise that they will find many different uses for them we also should help them to understand that certain things are used for particular purposes, so sticky tape is for sticking things, rather than for making into a ball, which might be a great idea for a game but if we play that game we need to use different resources! It is also important to help children to explore different areas of provision out of doors. Unless they are supported to strike out into different areas some children will return to the same ones day after day. If this happens then the play can become repetitive and low level and may exclude certain children who find it difficult to join in.

Optimising opportunities for play and learning outside

Every child is unique with their own experiences, interests and personalities which become clearer to us as we observe them. There will be the child who is an independent explorer and a child who wants attention most of the time perhaps afraid they may get forgotten if they don't regale us regularly with new information such as 'I'm going to my dad's house tonight'; 'My mummy's working'; 'I've got new shoes'; 'They won't let me play' and so on.

Understanding children's different needs is essential if we are going to help them make progress in the EYFS so trying to accommodate their different learning styles is something we need to take account of. Outdoor play is a boon for young children who need to be active most of the time because there is more space and no requirement to sit still and listen unless for a particular purpose such as listening to a story. Successfully managing play and learning out of doors is a particular skill because, left to their own devices, some children would spend all their days playing football, riding bikes, climbing slides or taking turns on swings. Yet although these things are an essential part of their experience they also need times when they can recover and do quieter, more restful activities such as exploring a sensory garden, watering plants or playing at picnics with a basket of food and some hungry 'guests'. For some children it will be necessary at times to engage in some less energetic activities, whilst for others it may be crucial to encourage them even to venture out the door. If a child is reticent about going outside, they may be encouraged if they know that there is something of particular interest going on such as a car wash with warm soapy water and big floppy sponges or a Bear Hunt with torches to hold and hot chocolate at the end of the search. To identify what your children like to do, scan your outdoor area at 15 minute intervals over an hour and complete Table 8.5, adding or substituting your own outdoor areas of provision to those listed. Then consider the number of children in each area during each of the four occasions you scan them.

Table 8.5 Use of Outdoor Areas of Provision

Areas of Provision	Number of children	Number of girls	Number of boys
Bikes, wheeled toys			
Balls, bats			
Throwing, catching			
Water			
Construction			
Climbing wall			
Water			
Sand			

Once you have established where children are spending their time outside, you can then consider the types of activities that engage their interests and what and how these can be built on through provision. This is the first step in providing for the different learning styles of children and is the start of a cycle as indicated in Table 8.6.

Table 8.6 Outdoor planning cycle

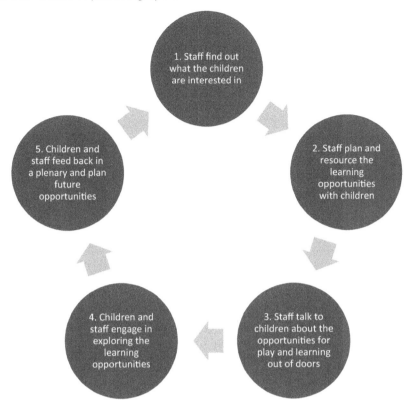

You may find that there are gender differences in the ways that children in your class play and in the activities they choose. Therefore, it's important to ensure that boys aren't put off taking part in imaginative play in the mud kitchen, for example, because this has been unofficially categorised as an activity for girls, or that girls are left to play around the edges of an area whilst boys dominate the space by playing football.

Having established the different ways that children choose to play outside, it is important to understand how to utilise this information so that what is on offer challenges children to try new things whilst reducing the time available to spend on repetitive activities such as goal scoring or making more and more potions. Beliefs about the value of supporting different styles of learning vary drastically. For those who subscribe to the view that these are important (as many schools do) three/four styles are proposed. This is described as the VAK model, which identifies Visual, Auditory and Kinaesthetic learners with some suggestion that a fourth category of logical/analytical learners is also to be considered. As the labels suggest, visual learners prefer to see things and remember by recording what they have learned, auditory learners prefer to learn by talking about or being told or shown how to do things, whilst the kinaesthetic group are hands-on learners who need to move to learn. The final group are thought to have a more mature logical system and are interested in exploring how and why things happen or what makes things work.

However, according to science, for example UCL's Centre for Educational Neuroscience, the existence of such categories of learners is a 'Neuro-myth'. They suggest that it is unproven in scientific studies that students fall into such groups and more worryingly, categorisation of students into these groups may be unhelpful in the long term.

What seems eminently clear when we observe them is that most young children seem to display the traits of all of the VAK groups simultaneously. However, perhaps the most compelling category they fit into is the Kinaesthetic group since they are more likely to have an urge to move and to touch things and to use all of their senses in finding out about the world and the things within it. Clearly, children are most likely to adopt ways of learning based on their experiences and therefore we should ensure that these are broad and diverse so that if they have a preferred style it is reflected in the opportunities on offer. For example, if a child wants to communicate something they have found out about a spider's web simply asking them to draw it may not be easy for them, whereas if they could recreate it with twigs and yarn, make it with clay or take a photograph of it you would probably be adjusting your expectations to accommodate the child's preferred learning style. By only slightly adjusting our thinking in this way, based on what we know about each child, we can encourage them to communicate their learning – the secret is having ways of encouraging this. The ways in which children respond to their experiences will depend on the open-mindedness, skills and ingenuity of the adults working with them. When children have a number of options they find the approach that best suits their way of responding and will derive far more pleasure (and learning) from doing it their own way, rather than having to do it the same way as everybody else.

So, providing for outdoor learning is as complex and extensive as providing for indoor learning. Some children will demonstrate their ease at being outside, becoming deeply involved in whatever catches their interest at a particular time.

Key takeaway

The outdoor environment can hold so much appeal for young children not only because of the scale and the freedom within it but also because it is constantly changing through the seasons and many different weather patterns. Helping children to enjoy the bounties of nature can lead towards them achieving most of the outcomes of the EYFS, so the value of outdoor play and learning should not be underestimated because 'real' learning can happen anywhere!

Sources

Ofsted school inspection handbook August 2018

- 'Teaching in the early years should not be taken to imply a "top down" or formal way of working. It is a broad term that covers the many different ways in which adults help young children learn. It includes their interactions with children during planned and child-initiated play and activities: communicating and modelling language, showing, explaining, demonstrating, exploring ideas, encouraging, questioning, recalling, and providing a narrative for what they are doing, facilitating and setting challenges. **It takes account of the equipment adults provide and the attention given to the physical environment, as well as the structure and routines of the day that establish expectations.** Integral to teaching is how practitioners assess what children know, understand and can do, as well as taking account of their interests and dispositions to learn (characteristics of effective learning), and how practitioners use this information to plan children's next steps in learning and monitor their progress...' (Page 58)

Statutory framework for the early years foundation stage: Setting the standards for learning, development and care for children from birth to five (2017)

'Providers must provide access to an outdoor play area or, if that is not possible, ensure that outdoor activities are planned and taken on a daily basis (unless circumstances make this inappropriate, for example unsafe weather conditions). Providers must follow their legal responsibilities under the Equality Act 2010 (for example, the provisions on reasonable adjustments).' (Page 30, paragraph 3.58)

Teachers' standards 2013

'TEACHING: A teacher must:

- Set high expectations which inspire, motivate and challenge pupils
- Impart knowledge and develop understanding through effective use of lesson time
- Promote a love of learning and children's intellectual curiosity
- Reflect systematically on the effectiveness of lessons and approaches to teaching
- Contribute to the design and provision of an engaging curriculum within the relevant subject area(s).' (Page 7)

9 Reaching out: Transition

Key Points

- Ensure that transition is on the school's agenda and is given the priority it deserves
- Invest time in developing a strong key person system to support families and their children throughout their time in the EYFS
- Have a clear plan for transition as children enter or move within the EYFS in school (nursery or Reception)
- Ensure that transition from Reception to Year 1 is seamless so that children continue to make progress

In this chapter you will be challenged to think about your school as an unknown and strange environment and you will also be encouraged to experience what it is like to be a newcomer in it – whether child or adult. Then you will be invited to explore the purpose of the role of the key person in the EYFS and to clarify your plans for children's transitions as they enter and leave the EYFS in your school.

Giving transition the priority it deserves

It can feel that the nursery or Reception class in school is a little like a conveyor belt with children arriving in September somewhat bewildered and then, just as their confusion has lifted, moving on in July. Because these years in school are so busy and there seems to be so much to fit in, it is small wonder that the positive value of a staged transition can sometimes be overlooked by leaders in schools. Yet, the role of school leaders in helping children become ready for school is critical, since it is recognised that: '*Children who have* [a] *positive start to school are well positioned to build a sense of belonging that promotes engagement in the educational environment*' (Dockett and Perry, 2017).

For children to settle well into school they need to feel a sense of acceptance and belonging and this will only happen when school leaders are proactive in making links to their feeder settings before the children are ready to move on to school.

Transition is also an issue which gives rise to considerable anxiety for families and children, particularly if it is seen as a 'one-off,' rather than as a period of adjustment. Research indicates '*that children… expect that school will be different from home or preschool, and that* they will be required to make adjustments to school. They expect to encounter large groups of people, learn at school, respond appropriately to school rules, and make friends' (Dockett and Perry, 2017). Understanding how major these adjustments are, not only for children but for their families, is essential. It is also important to ensure that any approach is underpinned by a well-thought-out policy which is complemented by clear plans that support seamless transition from one class to another, particularly when the move is into Key Stage One.

Whilst it is accepted that most children successfully move from stage to stage throughout school, it is also important to be aware that the lives of many children can be either positively or negatively affected, as a result of the way transition is managed. Indeed, an NFER review of the research literature which assessed the evidence from studies as well as the views of service users concluded: 'The majority of children and young people make successful educational transitions. Individuals who experience difficulties are more likely to be from vulnerable groups, including those from deprived backgrounds and those with special educational needs' (CEO, 2010). Therefore, we can assume that most schools do a very good job of managing transition. However, the same report indicates that younger children are another vulnerable group particularly at the end of the EYFS, stating: 'At the transition from early years foundation stage to key stage 1, children who are the youngest in their year have been found to experience more difficulties' (CEO, 2010).

Given the evidence, it is clear that transition is an important issue that schools should prioritise – not only the transition from primary to secondary school (a subject of vast amounts of research) but also for children starting school, moving classes within school and transferring from EYFS to Key Stage One. The latter is particularly significant currently because of greater prescription, especially in English and mathematics, for five- to six-year-olds in the National Curriculum (2014).

As a starting point for exploring the issue of transition both into, within and beyond the EYFS consider which of the good practice points in Table 9.1 are established, developing, on your radar, or are worthy of further consideration in relation to transition from preschool to school nursery or Reception classes.

When you have reviewed your current practice, you may wish to identify your school's strengths as well as areas for further consideration regarding transition.

A strong key person system

Just imagine, for a moment, that you had never walked through the doors of your school before or better still, remember when you walked in on the first day you started work there. Almost everybody was a stranger and you didn't know much about this new, unknown, interesting, yet strange environment. It's probably difficult to remember this unless you have only just started in a new school so perhaps some of the prompts in the form of questions you might have had but perhaps didn't like to ask, in Table 9.2, will help you to recall this transition period.

Table 9.1 Good practice in transition

Transition from preschool to school (nursery or Reception classes) *(since the majority of children attend preschool settings before school entry the issue of home to school has not been addressed here)*				
ISSUE	**Established**	**Developing**	**On the radar**	**Something to consider**
Transition to EYFS informs School Transition Policy				
Planning for September transition begins in previous Autumn term				
Planning for transition includes:				
Conferences with individual parents to identify child's needs and strengths				
Meeting with parents of cohort to discuss classes, uniform, staggered entry, expectations, lunchtime arrangements, etc.				
Meeting with parents of cohort to discuss approaches to teaching and learning, phonics, reading, writing, maths, homework, etc.				
Optional home visits by EYFS team members to meet children				
Series of play sessions for children and parents to visit classes				
Series of play sessions for children to stay without parent or carer				
Drop-in sessions for parents to discuss specific issues as they arise after parent/teacher conferences, e.g. a change in a child's health needs or in response to other worries or concerns				
Virtual tour of the classroom, toilets, outdoor area, etc., on the school's website				

ISSUE	Established	Developing	On the radar	Something to consider
Downloads on the school website that help children find out about the class they are going into, e.g. a class picture book: *Meet Fred and Felicity – the goldfish*, or a choose your favourite activity showing pictures of what's available in the outdoor area				
Liaison with feeder settings:				
Visits by school staff to feeder settings within reasonable reach				
Hosting visits from preschool feeder settings on fact-finding missions				
Sharing information with feeder settings about the school environment – may be in the form of a booklet which could be shared with children, containing pictures of staff, classrooms and outdoor areas				
Sharing information with feeder settings about school approach to teaching, e.g. how mark making is supported in school				
Inviting feeder setting staff to relevant continuing professional development sessions (CPD)				
Seeking and valuing information about children's learning from feeder settings at transfer and seeking clarification as necessary from them				
Reviewing transition practices and supporting transition by providing uniforms to feeder settings, for example				
Inviting feeder settings to events at school that recognise their valuable contributions to children's prior learning, e.g. an assembly where children are singing or acting out a story				

The list in Table 9.2 could go on endlessly so if you don't see one of your own queries (from when you were a newcomer) just add that to the list and respond according to how you solved the problem. When you have addressed the questions you may have a tiny taster of recalling what it feels like to be a newcomer in your school. However, the great advantage that you have over parents and children that come to your school is that you were selected on merit to become a member of the school workforce when you applied for a position there. That immediately gave you a head start in becoming familiar with the school, your colleagues and the rules and regulations that apply to you whilst you are working there.

Table 9.2 Becoming a stranger in your setting

Possible concern questions	If I asked myself any of these questions how did I find out the answers to them?
What time does the building open in the morning?	
When does the building close at night?	
Do I have to hand my planning in?	
If so, when?	
What are the arrangements about lunchtime for the children?	
Do teachers go out to bring their own class in?	
If so, when?	

Possible concern questions	If I asked myself any of these questions how did I find out the answers to them?
What happens about getting a drink if I'm on duty?	
Do people use any cup in the staffroom?	
Do I need to be on a rota for buying milk, washing up in the staffroom?	
My children's outdoor area is next to Y2 – do I need to keep them away from the windows?	
What will the caretaker say when he sees this mess?	
Are Reception children supposed to go into assembly? Why/why not?	
Who's who?	

Additionally, unlike many young children, you are able to formulate questions and know who to ask what – hence you wouldn't ask the caretaker whether the Reception children should go into assembly no more than you would ask one of the lunchtime supervisors who you should show your planning to. Simple, isn't it? Unless you are a three-, four- or five-year-old or an anxious parent who is uncertain about things you might never have dreamt of!

The kinds of anxieties that parents have about children starting at nursery or in a Reception class are discussed at length on websites such as Mumsnet™, which may be a useful source if you want to find out more about parents' worries. However, just so that this issue is not overlooked, consider how much better a parent would feel if planning for transition from preschool to school included some of the strategies set out in Table 9.1.

Now to children. Unlike adults, they are often unsure about what the question is as well as to whom they might address it because they don't know what they don't know! But they know inside themselves that school is going to be a big challenge and even if they have visited school before they may have never stayed there for a whole day. They may be excited and keen to start 'big school' at the same time as being unclear or unrealistic about what it involves. Add to that a PE bag to bring in one day and a reading bag to take home every day, new people (they don't yet know properly), new words they don't understand – think of 'assembly', 'equipment', 'apparatus', 'we're going to change now' – into what they may ask! So suddenly, an otherwise confident child may find that school is a very strange place where they don't understand the language – or the customs such as asking to go the toilet, hanging their clothes on a peg, wearing school uniform, walking indoors, speaking in turn and so on. And what is the biggest difference for a young child? It's the feeling of being on their own with no one they really know taking care of them, even when adults are very kind. Another factor that often impacts after a period of transition is that some children who were excited at the prospect of this new venture then wake up to the fact that going to school is a permanent measure, whereas although they may have looked forward to this big event in their lives they didn't fully appreciate that it would keep happening.

Research also shows that one of the greatest challenges for children who move from preschool to school is the differential in adult:child ratios. In addition to this, there is the difference in expectations (learning about being a pupil) and finally the sense of being a little fish in a big pool. Indeed, it has been argued that during transition children have to adjust not only to changes in environment and routines but also more fundamentally to 'social identity' (who they are, i.e. no longer a child at preschool but now a pupil) and new 'social networks' (having to make new relationships with different children and adults from those they already know).

Yet, if asked about them, adult:child ratios aren't something that children or parents think about very much, although parents are usually very concerned that their children should settle in and be happy at school. However, this issue is absolutely a concern for educators, not only because they know that children thrive when they feel confident and comfortable in a new situation but also because it makes sense in terms of continuity in learning. Also, because making it work successfully is enshrined in the legislation of the EYFS, in as much as it states that: *Each child must be assigned a key person… The key person must help ensure that every child's learning and care is tailored to meet their individual needs.*

The key person must seek to engage and support parents and/or carers in guiding their child's development at home. They should also help families engage with more specialist support if appropriate' (DfE, 2017:10).

Key takeaway

Therefore, it is clear that investing thought and time into the key person role and how it is to be facilitated is advisable. The majority of schools wisely provide the best adult:child ratios they can afford because leaders recognise that investing in the Reception year in school makes sense. Indeed, when the Teaching Schools Council consulted with a group of teachers, school leaders and academics to consider the most effective practice for mainstream, state-funded primary schools in England they stated: *'In our view, Reception is the most important year. Done well and properly invested in, it will provide pupils with a strong foundation for the rest of their time in school'* (TSC, 2016:37). It is not surprising therefore that many schools endeavour to limit class sizes and create more favourable ratios, particularly in Reception classes, going beyond the statutory 1:30 adult:child ratio requirement. Where this is the case the key person system usually works well. Where this is not the case it is likely to be more challenging and less satisfactory for all concerned: children, parents and professionals.

A successful key person system is based on two EYFS principles: positive relationships and enabling environments, visually: *'Children learn to be strong and independent through* **positive relationships***' and 'children learn and develop well in* **enabling environments***, in which their experiences respond to their individual needs and there is a strong partnership between practitioners and parents and/or carer'* (DfE, 2017). As can be seen from the above, relationships are of prime importance in enabling and facilitating children's development and learning throughout their first years until they reach the age of five (though clearly the importance of this continues throughout the school years).

How a key person is assigned to which child and family is a decision to be made by the school and the way this is planned is a whole school issue, strongly connected to its policies on working in partnership with parents. However, in the early stages of a child starting at a school it is important that children and parents are clear about who the adults are in the classroom and the roles they each play in the child's education. In addition, transition practice should go a long way towards reassuring children and parents about questions that they might have had but were, in the case of children, unable to ask, or, in the case of parents, felt they would look silly for even thinking of asking them! However, being aware of these issues will mean that schools can pre-empt many teething problems that starting school brings.

It is also worth considering adding the following guidance, published alongside the EYFS on the role of the key person, to your transition policy:

'It is helpful to us all, when in a strange situation, to have someone we can rely on to interpret unfamiliar experiences for us until we feel confident to manage the situation on our own. Even then, if we feel unwell, unsure or overwhelmed, knowing that there is someone there whom we can ask for help if necessary, is reassuring and can enable us to tackle something on our own that we might otherwise avoid. This is what key people do for their allocated group of children. Young children need to know that someone in particular keeps them 'in mind' while they are away from their parents' (Grenier et al., 2007).

Planning for transition as children enter the EYFS

If the previous section has chimed with your own experience then it will be clear to you that transition is not a one-off event that happens when Year 6 children visit their secondary school, providing an opportunity throughout the school for each child to spend a day in their new classroom and allowing for the new nursery and Reception children to visit for part of the day. An adage that comes to mind with transition is that it is '90 per cent preparation and only 10 per cent perspiration' if it is planned carefully. That is, a measured approach resolves most potential difficulties because transition is recognised as an adjustment process. How can we plan and prepare so that when children arrive in school we see them as eager, anticipative and keen to learn and make new friends? A recent report in Scotland on the international research indicates: *'Effective transition programmes incorporate three strands involving children, parents and teachers: helping children become familiarized with their new situation, informing parents about the school, and teachers being informed about children's development and past experiences'* (Evidence Request Bank Development Project, 2014).

The most important factors in any transition include positive relationships, open and clear communication, mutual respect between those involved and a sense of a shared enterprise or partnership working. There is some evidence to conclude that when child/teacher relationships are cordial children cope better than if these are unsatisfactory. The same is likely to be the case if the parent and teacher get along well or alternatively if they do not see eye to eye, for some reason. Therefore, it is crucial that teachers foster positive, respectful relationships with parents and children, alike. Similarly, it is also important that teachers support children to establish positive relationships with other adults and children in school. Helping a child to find a friend has been found to be one of the most important and effective things for boosting children's confidence. This is not only key because of the feelings of self-worth a child may gain as a result but also as an antidote to the feelings of being a small fish in a very big pool. When a child knows the names and faces of one or two significant others their own need for recognition is being met.

A major source of difficulty in relationships can be caused by mixed or confused messages being conveyed by one of the parties – so developing a policy that spells out clearly how the transition will be managed is essential and, in order to keep the policy current and workable, getting feedback on its effectiveness from parents and children who attended the class the previous year will be invaluable.

Some top tips from experts in the field have been presented in Table 9.3 as questions, supplemented by additional ideas (Evidence Request Bank Development Project, 2014), along with others based on practice in schools I know, to allow you to reflect on how you plan for transition.

Table 9.3 How you plan for transition

Things to consider	Your response	Next steps
Have you asked any preschool children what they want to know about your school?		
Have you asked children who started at your school last year or the year before what new children need to know?		
If you have a gradual admissions policy, how do you decide which children will start when?		
What are your aims for transition – how will you know when you have achieved them?		

Things to consider	Your response	Next steps
If you have a nursery, how do you manage to accommodate the different needs of children who are new to your school and those who are familiar with many aspects of it?		
How do you manage transition for children with older siblings at the school, compared with those who are the first family member to attend?		
Do you use multiple forms of information for parents such as brochures, stories, online material, electronic observation sharing?		
How do you encourage informal visits from parents?		
Do you offer a variety of transition activities, both formal and informal?		
Do you allow children to participate in activities with older children when they visit?		

Things to consider	Your response	Next steps
Do you offer a range of opportunities for parents to access based around what to expect during transition?		
Do you introduce parents to other parents whose children will be in the same class?		
Do you encourage older children to act as 'buddies' to younger children at times when they may feel anxious such as during lunchtime or events such as a theatre visit?		
How do you offer reassurance to parents who are new to schooling, that is, that don't have older children in school?		

Reception to year 1: A seamless transition

Ofsted has recently changed its views about ways of supporting a seamless transition from Reception into Year 1. This is because the prescribed learning in Year 1 has become 'out of kilter' (as a direct result of the increasing demands of the new National Curriculum, published in 2014) with what children are expected to know at the end of the EYFS.

Reflecting the thoughts of leaders in 41 'good' or 'outstanding' schools and feedback from more than 200 questionnaires, an Ofsted report tells us that *'foremost in leaders' minds was the need to prepare children for the demands of the years ahead by enabling them to become successful and self-motivated'* (Ofsted, 2017:12) adding further that amongst the factors deemed important for the Reception Year in school were the following to…

1. *'prepare children for the demands of Year 1, including the increased expectations of the 2014 National Curriculum*
2. *secure the essential skills of reading, writing and mathematics, as the gatekeepers for successful learning across all other subjects*
3. *start quickly, from the first week of the new academic year*
4. *build on children's learning from the end of nursery and/or preschool*
5. *instil a day-to-day routine so that children feel safe, secure and happy*
6. *connect to the wider school community through Reception children's participation in whole-school events and celebrations, setting the rules and expectations early on for behaviour in the school as a whole*
7. *develop children's confidence, concentration and ability to listen and follow instructions*
8. *continue the effective working relationships forged with parents*
9. *generate a love of learning and an enjoyment of school'* (Ofsted, 2017:12).

The list might have made happier reading had the final three factors: numbers 7, 8 and 9 above been placed at the top, followed by numbers 5 and 4 whilst omitting numbers 1, 2, 3 and 6. The reason for suggesting this is because children of four and five years of age are exceedingly different from one another in their development and indeed, more significantly in their ages – and age really does matter where young children are concerned since, as we are all aware, the range in age at the start of the Reception year is significantly greater (relative to life span) than at any other time in a child's school life. The abridged list would have made much more sense had it looked like this:

- *'generate a love of learning and an enjoyment of school*
- *continue the effective working relationships forged with parents*
- *develop children's confidence, concentration and ability to listen and follow instructions*
- *instil [introduce] a day-to-day routine so that children feel safe, secure and happy*
- *build on children's learning from the end of nursery and/or preschool'.*

The omission of points at 1, 2, 3 and 6 does not mean that there would be any reduction in learning. Rather it indicates that early years education is not a transmission model but a process based on relationships of care and concern. So, *starting quickly from the first week of the academic year* is redundant since teaching does start from the first hour of the first day in school, as it involves introducing children to one another, the classroom and the outdoor areas as well as the toilets, the dinner room and hall; in addition to a myriad of adults and bigger children, together with all the rules and experiences that have to be explained and understood.

Securing the essential skills of reading, writing and mathematics is something that happens currently in nursery and Reception classes at a level appropriate to the ages and stages of the young children who attend them. Linking to this is point 1, which is the idea that Reception class is a preparation for the next class. This is both true and false, since it should not be considered primarily as preparation for the next stage because it is an important stage in its own right. The conflation in the report of *'setting the rules and expectations for behaviour'* with not *'connecting to whole-school events and celebrations'* suggests that the decision not to involve Reception children in assemblies at the start of the school year implies some sort of deviousness which is, of course, far from the case. Rather, it derives from recognition that for very young children assemblies are usually overlong and irrelevant at the start of the year when what they need most in order to settle in well is the predictability of their new classroom environment and the routines of the day within it. Finally, the desire to *'prepare children for the demands of Year 1, including the increased expectations of the 2014 National Curriculum'* reflects the desire for a different framework from the current EYFS: the statutory document.

What then are school leaders to do in the face of this dichotomy – between the requirements of a statutory framework and the need to justify a school's performance? Clearly, the answer must be a pragmatic response which ensures that the statutory duty is followed and children's needs are met appropriately. Many schools achieve this balance very effectively, recognising the importance of transition between the play-based approach to learning in the EYFS and a more formal, though still play-based approach in Year 1. A further consideration is that the Early Years Profile (EYFSP) Guidance states: *'Practitioners and year 1 teachers should work together to ensure that a child's transition between the EYFS and year 1 is seamless'* (STA, 2017:17). In the following table are some questions and ideas that are or have been used in local authorities and schools. These give an indication of how an effective transition can be achieved. Many of these ideas were also endorsed by Ofsted, prior to the publication of the document previously discussed). You are invited to respond to the ideas in Table 9.4.

Table 9.4 Seamless transition: EYFS to Key Stage One

Issue	Current position	Queries or comments
Curriculum		
Do you have an up to date Transition Policy?		

Issue	Current position	Queries or comments
Have you identified commonalities between the EYFS and aspects of the Y1 curriculum?		
How do you promote continuity in the curriculum between YR and Y1?		
Do you plan opportunities for enquiry learning in Y1? What are these?		
Assessment strategies		
Does assessment in Y1 involve observations?		
Is planning for learning in Y1 informed by observations and ongoing assessment?		
Do teachers (YR and Y1) share perspectives on children's learning through observing practice in each other's classes?		

Issue	Current position	Queries or comments
Planning strategies		
Is the EYFS Profile data used to directly inform planning in Y1?		
What arrangements are made in terms of the different needs of children with the outcome of 'Emerging' in Y1, especially in view of the narrowing the gap agenda?		
Do you plan collaboratively with Y1 colleagues from the end of the Summer term into the Autumn term, for children who will be moving into Y1?		
How do you plan to ensure there is continuity from Reception to Y1, bearing in mind the greater demands of the National Curriculum?		

Based on Developing Successful Transitions Year R to Year One, Gloucestershire Children and Young People's Services

In conclusion, it is important to consider that as findings from research show: *'The process of transition may be viewed as one of adaptation… the best adaptation takes place where conditions are similar, communication is encouraged and the process of change takes place gradually over time'* (NFER, 2005). Aiming for this may make the difference between a child's success or failure throughout their school lives.

Sources

Ofsted school inspection handbook August 2018

- 'Integral to teaching is how practitioners assess what children know, understand and can do, as well as taking account of their interests and dispositions to learn (characteristics of effective learning), and how practitioners use this information to plan children's next steps in learning and monitor their progress.' (Page 58)

Statutory framework for the early years foundation stage: Setting the standards for learning, development and care for children from birth to five (2017)

'As children grow older, and as their development allows, it is expected that the balance will gradually shift towards more activities led by adults, to help children prepare for more formal learning, ready for Year 1.' (Page 9, paragraph 1.8)

Teachers' standards 2013

'TEACHING: A teacher must:

- Set high expectations which inspire, motivate and challenge pupils
- Impart knowledge and develop understanding through effective use of lesson time
- Promote a love of learning and children's intellectual curiosity
- Reflect systematically on the effectiveness of lessons and approaches to teaching
- Contribute to the design and provision of an engaging curriculum within the relevant subject area(s).' (Page 7)

Early years foundation stage profile 2018 handbook

'EYFS profile data is used to:

- support a smooth transition to key stage 1 (KS1) by informing the professional dialogue between EYFS and KS1 teachers
- help year 1 teachers plan an effective, responsive and appropriate curriculum that will meet the needs of all children'. (Page 10)

'2.5 Transition to year 1

Practitioners and year 1 teachers should work together to ensure that a child's transition between the EYFS and year 1 is seamless. Early years practitioners should make sure children's experiences in the final year of the EYFS are valuable in themselves, and prepare the ground for year 1. It is important that year 1 builds on the successful principles and approach encapsulated in the EYFS.

It is crucial that EYFS practitioners and year 1 teachers are given time to discuss and expand on the information presented in the EYFS profile. In particular, the characteristics of effective learning narratives will give teachers significant details about each child's learning and development. The narratives must feature in conversations between practitioners and teachers.

Practitioners may provide additional information about each child's attainment to help teachers plan an effective curriculum and make provision for all children. Decisions about this additional information should be made by each setting and reflect the characteristics and requirements of that setting. This will enable the year 1 teacher to have a fully rounded picture of the attainment of each child in order to plan the curriculum. Year 1 teachers should be involved in EYFS profile moderation so that they understand the judgements made by early years practitioners.' (Page 17)

10 Evaluation: Internal and external

Key Points

- Continuously develop your own vision and values and check out how they are evident in practice
- Be aware of Thorndike's 'halo effect' and the importance of first impressions
- Assertively review your own practice and be confident in your knowledge of the EYFS, the Ofsted framework and the Teachers' Standards
- Feed your self-evaluation into both internal (within school) and external evaluations

Living by your own vision and values

In a world where there is constant evaluation of practice, it is important to continuously develop your own vision and values so that what you do in practice accurately reflects these. When teachers are less experienced their vision may be focused, in the early days, on survival of their NQT year but as they become more proficient their horizons often expand as they aspire to become the best they can be. With this development, there emerges a recognition of the reasons that guided their choice to become a teacher and the philosophy that underpins their thinking – the latter often informed by their own 'story', that is, the events or ideals that motivated them to take this particular career path.

Whatever drew each of us to become teachers is part of our core belief system which together with other implicit or explicit beliefs creates our mindset and becomes a measure of our values. Often, it is only when we are confronted with ideas that challenge our thinking that we pause to consider where we stand on a particular issue, for example, one that consistently challenges many people is whether young children in the EYFS should be taught cursive writing. Some schools use this approach and feel it is very successful as a method, whilst other schools find the idea abhorrent for innumerable reasons. Yet children the world over learn to represent their thoughts using a range of scripts, some of which even as adults we might find challenging to learn. However, because schools may choose which approach they prefer, most adhere to the views of the majority and adopt their preferred method unless and until research or some specific directive changes their thinking.

When thinking about your own philosophy, Table 10.1 is a useful reminder to help you reflect on the 16 principles on which the EYFS was founded.

Clearly the EYFS principles are given, and must be adhered to. However, our more fundamental beliefs about how children learn, how to meet children's needs and what is an appropriate curriculum make greater demands on our standpoint since they provide a perspective on our own values. Consider whether you agree or disagree with the points in Table 10.2 and then the extent to which they are demonstrated in your EYFS practice.

Table 10.1 EYFS Principles

A Unique Child	Positive Relationships	Enabling Environments	Learning and Development
1.1 Child Development Babies and children develop in individual ways and at varying rates. Every area of development – physical, cognitive, linguistic, spiritual, social and emotional – is equally important.	**2.1 Respecting Each Other** Every interaction is based on caring professional relationships and respectful acknowledgement of the feelings of children and their families.	**3.1 Observation, Assessment and Planning** Babies and young children are individuals first, each with a unique profile of abilities. Schedules and routines should flow with the child's needs. All planning starts with observing children in order to understand and consider their current interests, development and learning.	**4.1 Play and Exploration** Children's play reflects their wide ranging and varied interests and preoccupations. In their play children learn at their highest level. Play with peers is important for children's development.
1.2 Inclusive Practice The diversity of individuals and communities is valued and respected. No child or family is discriminated against.	**2.2 Parents as Partners** Parents are children's first and most enduring educators. When parents and practitioners work together in early years settings, the results have a positive impact on children's development and learning.	**3.2 Supporting Every Child** The environment supports every child's learning through planned experiences and activities that are challenging but achievable.	**4.2 Active Learning** Children learn best through physical and mental challenges. Active learning involves other people, objects, ideas and events that engage and involve children for sustained periods.

A Unique Child	Positive Relationships	Enabling Environments	Learning and Development
1.3 Keeping Safe Young children are vulnerable. They develop resilience when their physical and psychological wellbeing is protected by adults.	**2.3 Supporting Learning** Warm, trusting relationships with knowledgeable adults support children's learning more effectively than any amount of resources.	**3.3 The Learning Environment** A rich and varied environment supports children's learning and development. It gives them the confidence to explore and learn in secure and safe, yet challenging, indoor and outdoor spaces.	**4.3 Creativity and Critical Thinking** When children have opportunities to play with ideas in different situations and with a variety of resources, they discover connections and come to new and better understandings and ways of doing things. Adult support in this process enhances their ability to think critically and ask questions.
1.4 Health and Wellbeing Children's health is an integral part of their emotional, mental, social, environmental and spiritual wellbeing and is supported by attention to these aspects.	**2.4 Key Person** A key person has special responsibilities for working with a small number of children, giving them the reassurance to feel safe and cared for and building relationships with their parents.	**3.4 The Wider Context** Working in partnership with other settings, other professionals and with individuals and groups in the community supports children's development and progress towards the outcomes of Every Child Matters: being healthy, staying safe, enjoying and achieving, making a positive.	**4.4 Areas of Learning and Development** The Early Years Foundation Stage (EYFS) is made up of six areas of Learning and Development. All areas of Learning and Development are connected to one another and are equally important. All areas of Learning and Development are underpinned by the Principles of the EYFS.

DfE (2017), Statutory Framework For the Early Years Foundation Stage: Setting the Standards for Learning, Development and Care For Children From Birth To Five

Table 10.2 Putting the EYFS principles into practice

Principle	Agree	Disagree	Established	Developing	On my radar	Something to consider
Children learn through:						
First-hand experiences						
Trial and error						
Repetition and practice						
Observing and imitating others						
Listening						
Talking						
Reflecting						
Interaction with others (adults or children)						
Making choices						
Recalling and remembering						
Following ideas or interests						
Returning to ideas or interests						
Seeing skills modelled						
The influence of the environment:						
Children know where to find things and where to return them to						
Children can exercise independence and choice because resources are easily accessible						

Principle	Agree	Disagree	Established	Developing	On my radar	Something to consider
Displays show the processes in children's work rather than simply focusing on the end product						
Enhancements are intriguing and invite children to use their senses in order to feel, smell, touch, taste or listen						
The freshness and appeal of each area is constantly 'a work in progress' so that children frequently encounter familiar things in new and different ways						
There is no 'one way' and open-ended resources can be used inventively, e.g. a mop might be for cleaning the floor but can be used to make a pattern on the concrete, creating a trail for another child to follow						
Care of the environment is discussed with children and solutions about the best way to care for things are agreed by adults and children together						
The curriculum:						
Provides a springboard to learning						
Is structured around the distinct needs of the children from this school and this community						
Is planned flexibly and is structured appropriately						
Allows children to explore their own interests						
Leads into areas a child might never discover by chance						
Comprises every action and interaction throughout the day						

Principle	Agree	Disagree	Established	Developing	On my radar	Something to consider
Is inclusive of all families, recognising the different needs and challenges for the most vulnerable						
Is constantly reviewed to ensure that it is appropriate for all children, e.g. a 'boy heavy' class						
Relationships:						
Everybody deserves and receives equal respect						
Create a strong sense of care for one another and the environment						
Provide positive role models about communicating respectfully and resolving conflict through discussion and reflection						
Each child and family have a key person who supports the child in school and helps the family support their child's learning at home						
Relationships create the emotional environment that enables children to grow in confidence knowing that others will support them to be the best they can be						

Table 10.2 may reveal a gap between your beliefs and your practice which is likely to be the case for all but the most diligent of us since it is not always easy to put our principles into practice. Therefore, it may be worth developing your own vision statement about your beliefs. Try to make this simple and direct and focused on your beliefs and children's needs. You may want to think about the following statements in Table 10.3 as prompts to help you begin.

Table 10.3 Vision statements

I/We believe…	
That parents are children's first educators and that by working together we can enable children to become the best they can be.	That every child is a competent learner.
That every child deserves the best we can offer so that they can develop and learn to their full potential.	That children learn during every moment of the day and from everything that happens whether that is planned or unplanned.
That learning takes place both indoors and out of doors – classrooms do not need to have walls and there are no barriers to learning when children are engaged and motivated.	That the curriculum should meet all their needs including those for movement, enquiry-based learning and for a calm and reassuring routine.
That first-hand experiences provide children with the enthusiasm to find their interests and pursue their curiosity.	That assessment is an integral part of the teaching process which leads to new learning.
That evidence of children's learning is gathered and documented in such a way that learning is made visible for children, their families and for all who are involved in their education.	That the curriculum is a springboard into a menu of good things for children to explore and experience so that they remain motivated and excited to learn and develop knowledge, understanding, skills and imagination.

If, having read these statements you are inspired to write your own vision statement begin by inviting every member of your team to contribute to it, then share and display it so that it becomes central to your practice. Ensure though that you review it regularly so that you always operate from these first principles.

The halo effect

According to business leaders, 'The "halo effect"' occurs 'when one trait of a person or thing is used to make an overall judgment of that person or thing. It supports rapid decisions, even if biased ones' and it works in both positive and negative directions. This is on the basis that 'if you like one aspect of something, you'll have a positive predisposition toward everything about it' and 'if you dislike one aspect of something, you'll have a negative predisposition toward everything about it.' So, since we know that first impressions are significant what should we be alert to when considering how we, our learning environment and our practice might be judged by others? Clearly, judgements may be made about our verbal and non-verbal communication or our openness, self-confidence and enthusiasm; as well as the quality of our relationships with children and adults and the care we put into creating a safe and emotionally warm environment which nurtures children and their learning. All of these can be fostered through feeling we are on solid ground. In other words, being conversant with the requirements of the EYFS allows us to feel confidence in knowing that what we are doing meets the statutory requirements. Similarly, familiarity with the relevant part of the Ofsted framework can empower us to take control of the agenda whilst a good grasp of the Teachers' Standards allows us to have clarity about expectations for our conduct, teaching and learning.

The EYFS (DfE, 2017) is a document of only 37 pages, half focusing on the principles, the learning and development requirements and the assessment arrangements, the rest focusing on the safeguarding and welfare requirements. How well do you know both sections? Are you more familiar with one than another? Being familiar with the whole document is essential if you are to feel confident about your role as a facilitator of young children's learning. As you develop a rationale for your practice (this will change over time because you are a reflective practitioner) continue to identify how it is consistent with the four principles in the EYFS, visually:

'Four guiding principles should shape practice in early years settings. These are:

- *every child is a unique child, who is constantly learning and can be resilient, capable, confident and self-assured*

- *children learn to be strong and independent through positive relationships*

- *children learn and develop well in enabling environments, in which their experiences respond to their individual needs and there is a strong partnership between practitioners and parents and/or carers*

- *children develop and learn in different ways (see "the characteristics of effective teaching and learning" at paragraph 1.9) and at different rates. The framework covers the education and care of all children in early years provision, including children with special educational needs and disabilities'* (DfE, 2017:6).

Sharing these principles is a good reminder for other adults who may be less familiar or committed to them than you. Perhaps you might want to invite parents at transition sessions to explain how the first principle describes aspects of their child's development: *'every child is a unique child, who is constantly learning and can be resilient, capable, confident and self-assured'* (DfE, 2017:6). Or, you may wish to create a display at the start of term focusing on the uniqueness of each child, showing their determination, persistence, skills and confidence as they start out on their EYFS journey with you.

Reference to the second principle may explain to parents and colleagues the importance of the key person role and why practices such as buddying or friendship benches are important to all children, but especially to the youngest children, who need the support of everybody in the school as they progress through school since *'children learn to be strong and independent through positive relationships'* (DfE, 2017:6).

The third principle *'children learn and develop well in enabling environments, in which their experiences respond to their individual needs and there is a strong partnership between practitioners and parents and/or carers'* (DfE, 2017:6) is a key consideration in the EYFS in as much as it tells us that working together with other practitioners and with parents is fundamental to children's success.

The last principle, *'children develop and learn in different ways… and at different rates'* (DfE, 2017:6), reminds us that development is non-linear and therefore we should not compare children or expect them to develop in the same way as their peers and furthermore, because the EYFS is inclusive, it applies to every child.

Having reflected on these, consider ways that you put them into practice and what factors compromise them if they are not seen as fundamental by all influencers in your school. Identify what actions you could take to promote the principles effectively.

If you are unsure about which factors might risk compromising any principle think about issues that you face currently but might not question, for example principle two (retaining all staff when there is a shortage elsewhere in school) might compromise the need for each child to have a key person, or expecting every child to eat lunch in the dinner hall, attend assembly or go to the toilet independently at the start of term might risk principle three which focuses on the importance of responding to children's individual needs. Once you have completed the matrix in Table 10.4 you will be able to see the strengths and weaknesses of your approach in relation to each of the principles. If you can identify areas for development you could list these in the column: 'Further actions to promote the principle'.

Familiarity with the Ofsted framework is a necessary read for everybody but once this is done and you are aware of the detail of the evaluation schedule, particular attention should be paid to the section *'Inspecting the effectiveness of the early years provision: quality and standards'* (Ofsted, 2018:64). This section sets out the areas for judging the early years:

- *'the effectiveness of leadership and management*
- *the quality of teaching, learning and assessment*
- *how well the provision contributes to children's personal development, behaviour and welfare*
- *outcomes for children'* (Ofsted, 2018:64).

Consider the statements in Table 10.5 taken from the Ofsted handbook and record in the evidence column any actions or strategies you currently do to achieve the quality required. If there are any gaps in your provision and practice make a note in the 'Next Steps' column to identify ways to prepare to demonstrate improvements.

Table 10.4 Retaining the EYFS principles

Principle	How this principle is put into practice	Factors that risk compromising this principle	Further actions to promote the principle
1. Every child is a unique child, who is constantly learning and can be resilient, capable, confident and self-assured.			
2. Children learn to be strong and independent through positive relationships			
3. Children learn and develop well in enabling environments, in which their experiences respond to their individual needs and there is a strong partnership between practitioners and parents and/or carers			
4. Children develop and learn in different ways ... and at different rates			

Table 10.5 Ofsted definition of teaching: Evidence

Inspectors will consider	Evidence	Next steps
The rigour and effectiveness of systems to drive improvement, including:		
- monitoring the quality of provision and children's outcomes		
- the professional development of staff		
- evaluation of the impact of actions taken		
- setting ambitious targets		
How effectively leaders use additional funding, including the early years pupil premium where applicable, and measure its impact on narrowing gaps in children's outcomes		
The effectiveness of safeguarding procedures		
How well teaching nurtures, engages and motivates children and promotes their sense of achievement and commitment to learning		
The breadth of the curriculum and how well it is based on accurate assessment of children's learning and development, so that activities and experiences meet their needs		
The quality and impact of phonics teaching		
How well all staff work with parents, engage them in their children's learning and keep them informed about their children's achievements and progress		

Inspectors will consider	Evidence	Next steps
Children's enjoyment of learning, including their participation and willingness to make choices and decisions, and the extent to which children are active and inquisitive learners who are creative and think critically		
How well children behave, cooperate and share with each other, make friends, respect each other's differences and build their understanding and respect for different families, people and communities beyond their immediate experience		
The extent to which children behave in ways that are safe, understand how to stay safe and show that they feel safe		
The proportions of children who have made typical or better progress from their starting points, including pupils who have special educational needs and/or disabilities and the most able		
The attainment of children at the end of Reception compared with early years foundation stage profile national figures, including the proportion that achieve a good level of development, particularly in terms of how well children are prepared for key stage 1		
Whether outcomes are consistent across areas of learning, particularly in the prime areas and the specific areas of literacy and mathematics		
How quickly disadvantaged children, and any groups that are underachieving, are catching up		

When you have completed this you will have a clear view of how well your provision and practice are meeting the required standards for Ofsted inspection. Clearly, on its own, this is not sufficient since, alongside this, your teaching should be at least good if not outstanding and all other areas referred to in the descriptors for Outstanding and/or Good in the effectiveness of the early years provision should be evident. Though, as is the case with the table, these are not intended as a check list although they do, together with the description of teaching (referred to in Chapter 5), shape expectations.

The Teachers' Standards are something you will be very familiar with if you have trained to become a teacher since 2012 and if this is not the case you will have focused on aspects of them in your performance management discussions. The standards are brief and the preamble states that:

'Teachers make the education of their pupils their first concern, and are accountable for achieving the highest possible standards in work and conduct. Teachers act with honesty and integrity; have strong subject knowledge, keep their knowledge and skills as teachers up-to-date and are self-critical; forge positive professional relationships; and work with parents in the best interests of their pupils' (DfE, 2013:7).

The standards are as follows:

'A teacher must:

1. *Set high expectations which inspire, motivate and challenge pupils*
2. *Promote good progress and outcomes by pupils*
3. *Demonstrate good subject and curriculum knowledge*
4. *Plan and teach well-structured lessons*
5. *Adapt teaching to respond to the strengths and needs of all pupils*
6. *Make accurate and productive use of assessment*
7. *Manage behaviour effectively to ensure a good and safe learning environment*
8. *Fulfil wider professional responsibilities'* (DfE, 2013:7–9).

The standards act as a good reminder of much of what has already been discussed in this book and keeping them in mind is essential if your self-evaluation is to be successful.

Linking self-evaluation to school evaluation

The point and purpose of self-evaluation at a personal level is essentially about developing and maintaining both self-belief and motivation in our work. This drive towards continuous improvement is the fuel that makes us want to do new things, try different approaches and learn from others. As indicated, it is also an essential part of our role as a teacher to undertake 'Appropriate self-evaluation' so whilst at one level it is a choice, at another level showing that we are reflective and 'self-critical' is a necessary part of being a teacher in schools.

Key takeaway

The self-evaluation you undertake is like a tributary to a river which is the school's own self-evaluation document. Together with records of performance management discussions, lesson observations, learning walks and continuing professional development records the whole should come together around a narrative that tells the school's story of how it is focused on the particular needs of its community, families and children and how the curriculum enables children to make progress relative to their very varied starting points.

As with the rest of the education system outcomes are paramount when any evaluation is made of the success either of an educational phase or of the whole school. That is why it is important to know your data and to be able to refer to it confidently in meetings with phase leaders, subject leaders and other colleagues as well as any external agencies who may wish to discuss this with you. To support such discussions it would be useful, as a minimum, to have the following information at your fingertips:

Table 10.6 Knowing your data

Useful information	Updated					
	Autumn 1	Autumn 2	Winter 1	Winter 2	Spring 1	Spring 2
Number of children on roll						
Gender balance: Number of boys						
Gender balance: Number of girls						
Number of children born in winter*						
Number of children born in spring**						

	Autumn 1	Autumn 2	Winter 1	Winter 2	Spring 1	Spring 2
Number of children born in summer***						
Number of children for whom English is an additional language						
Number of looked after children						
Number of children with additional needs and/or disabilities						
Number of children in receipt of Early Years Pupil Premium						
Number of children who entered school after the start of the academic year						

* Outcomes for winter born children tend to be higher than those of their spring or summer born peers

** Children born in springtime tend to achieve better than those born in summer and less well than those born in the winter

*** Children born in summer tend to achieve less well than those born in winter or spring

In addition to the factual information measured in Table 10.6 it is also useful to be able to confidently discuss the following topics:

- **Baseline information** (based on Early Years Outcomes is sufficient, it is not necessary to use a specific scheme) – numbers and percentage of children that started school at the age-related expectation (ARE), below or above the ARE, in each of the *seven areas of the EYFS*

- Numbers and percentage of children that started school at the age-related expectation (ARE), below or above the ARE in each of the *three prime areas of the EYFS*

- Numbers and percentage of children that started school at the age-related expectation (ARE), below or above the ARE in each of the *four specific areas of the EYFS*

- **Outcomes at the end of the EYFS from previous years** (based on the Early Years Profile) – numbers and percentage of children that ended the school year at the age-related expectation (ARE), below or above the ARE in *each of the seven areas of the EYFS*

- **Outcomes at the end of the EYFS from previous years** (based on the Early Years Profile) – numbers and percentage of children that ended the Years Profile who achieved the *Good Level of Development* in the EYFS, that is, that achieved at least the expected outcome in each of the *three prime areas and in the areas of Literacy and Mathematics*

- **Analysis of current year groups** and the extent to which the current cohort or groups within the cohort are *on track to achieve the GLD*, together with *information about any interventions* in place to narrow the gap between the most and least advantaged groups.

When this information is available you will be in a position to consider trends in your data story so that you can explore reasons for particular successes or look at areas where outcomes are inconsistent or less successful. Analysing your data can then help you to consider whether you need to plan such things as a longer or better induction period at the end of the academic year when new children are preparing to join your school, or whether you should invite parents to additional sessions so that they are fully informed about how to help their child's learning at home. The most important thing is to know what the data is telling you and then to be able to demonstrate that you are addressing any issues which have emerged in the best way possible.

Change is always happening and the key survival technique in the face of change is adaptability, so whether the Ofsted framework or the ELGs change, the most important thing we can do, if we are to succeed, is to have a clear understanding of what is involved and a readiness to adapt. This does not mean compromising our values and beliefs, it merely means adjusting what we do to synergise with the latest developments because those engaging in effective pedagogy and practice will always place the needs and development of the child at the centre of what they do and have as their guide the EYFS principles (referred to in this book). Finally, the way we can make early education better for children is to continually reflect on what we are doing so that we can find new ways to interest, engage, motivate and inspire them to develop a love of life and learning. Children are our future and they deserve the very best we can offer – everyday!

Sources

Teachers' standards 2013

'Similarly, headteachers (or appraisers) should assess teachers' performance against the standards to a level that is consistent with what should reasonably be expected of a teacher in the relevant role and at the relevant stage of their career (whether they are a newly qualified teacher (NQT), a mid-career teacher, or a more experienced practitioner).' (Page 3)

'The Preamble summarises the values and behaviour that all teachers must demonstrate throughout their careers. Part 1 comprises the Standards for Teaching; Part 2 comprises the Standards for Professional and Personal Conduct.' (Page 4)

'**Appropriate self-evaluation, reflection and professional development activity is critical** to improving teachers' practice at all career stages. The standards set out clearly the key areas in which a teacher should be able to assess his or her own practice, and receive feedback from colleagues.' (Page 4)

References

4Children (2015), 'What to expect, when?', available at: www.4Children.org.uk

Andreae, G. and Parker-Rees, G. (2000), *Giraffes Can't Dance*. London: Orchard Books.

Barker, F. (2017), 'Learning styles in children', *kidspot*, avaiable at: https://www.kidspot.com.au/school/primary/learning-and-behaviour/learning-styles-in-children/news-story/2c188e7d8ca8d273b2f441fcae6ae1ba

Burnett, D. (2016), *The Idiot Brain: A Neuroscientist Explains What Your Head is Really Up To*. London: Faber & Faber.

Centre for Educational Neuroscience (2016), 'Children have different learning styles', available at: www.educationalneuroscience.org.uk/neuromyth-or-neurofact/children-have-different-learning-styles/

Connell, G. and McCarthy, C. (2014), *A Moving Child is a Learning Child: How the body teaches the brain to think*. Minneapolis: Free Spirit Publishing Inc.

Cooper, H. (1999), *Pumpkin Soup*. London: Random House Children's Books.

Department for Education (2013a), 'Teachers' Standards: Guidance for school leaders, school staff and governing bodies', available at: www.gov.uk/government/publications/teachers-standards

Department for Education (2013b), 'Early years outcomes: A non-statutory guide for practitioners and inspectors to help inform understanding of child development through the early years', available at: www.foundationyears.org.uk/files/2012/03/Early_Years_Outcomes.pdf

Department for Education (2014), 'Special educational needs and disability: A guide for parents and carers', available at: www.gov.uk/government/publications/send- guide-for-parents-and-carers

Department for Education (2017), 'Statutory framework for the early years foundation stage: Setting the standards for learning, development and care for children from birth to five', available at: www.foundationyears.org.uk/files/2017/03/eyfs_statutory_framework_2017.pdf

Department for Education/Department of Health (2015), 'Special educational needs and disability code of practice: 0 to 25 years: Statutory guidance for organisations which work with and support children and young people who have special educational needs or disabilities', available at: www.gov.uk/government/publications/send-code-of-practice-0-to-25

Department of Health and Social Care (2011), 'UK physical activity guidelines', available at: www.gov.uk/government/publications/uk-physical-activity-guidelines

Dockett, S. and Perry, B. (2014), 'Continuity of Learning: A resource to support effective transition to school and school age care'. Canberra: Australian Government Department of Education.

Dockett, S., and Perry, B. (2017), 'The Role of Schools and Communities in Children's School Transition. Australia: Murray School of Education, Charles Sturt University, available at: www.child-encyclopedia.com/sites/default/files/textes-experts/en/814/the-role-of-schools-and-communities-in-childrens-school-transition.pdf

Early Education (2012), 'Development Matters in the Early Years Foundation Stage', available at www.foundationyears.org.uk/wp-content/uploads/2012/03/Development-Matters-FINAL-PRINT-AMENDED.pdf

Evidence Request Bank Development Project (2014), 'Transition to primary school: What factors affect children's transition to primary school, and are there factors which mean some children manage better than others? What can help in managing transitions and what are the barriers for services and families?', available at: www.crfr.ac.uk/assets/ERB-Transition-to-primary-school-FINAL.pdf

Grenier, J., Elfer, P., Manning Morton, J., Wilson, D. and Dearnley, K. (?), 'Guidance: the key person in reception classes and small nursery settings', available at: http://dnn.essex.gov.uk/Portals/49/Documents/EYFS/Nat%20Strat%20Guidance%20the%20key%20person%20in%20reception%20classes%20and%20small%20nursery%20settings.pdf

Langston, A. (2014), *Facilitating Children's Learning in the EYFS*. Maidenhead: Open University Press.

Leicestershire County Council (?), 'Outdoor Learning', available at: https://resources.leicestershire.gov.uk/sites/resource/files/field/pdf/2017/1/12/outdoor_learning_publication-2.pdf

Nielsen, J. and Cardello, J. (2013), 'The Halo Effect', *NN/g Nielsen Norman Group*, available at: www.nngroup.com/articles/halo-effect/

NASUWT The Teachers' Union (2015), 'The Common Inspection Framework: maintained schools and academies: Guidance for Teachers'.

Ofsted (2017), 'Bold beginnings: The Reception curriculum in a sample of good and outstanding primary schools', available at: www.gov.uk/government/publications/reception- curriculum-in-good-and-outstanding-primary-schools-bold-beginnings'

Ofsted (2018), 'School inspection handbook: Handbook for inspecting schools in England under section 5 of the Education Act 2005', available at: https://assets.publishing.service.gov.uk/government/uploads/system/uploads/attachment_data/file/730127/School_inspection_handbook_section_5_270718.pdf

Potter, B. (2002), *The Tale of Squirrel Nutkin*. London: Frederick Warne.

Reggio Emilia (2015), 'The 100 Languages', available at: https://reggioemilia2015.weebly.com/the-100-languages.html

Sharp, C., Morris, M., Marshall, H., Evans, K., George, N. and White, K. (2010), 'Ensuring that all children and young people make sustained progress and remain fully engaged through transitions between key stages'. London: Centre for Excellence and Outcomes in Children and Young People's Services (C4EO), available at: www.nfer.ac.uk/publications/11107

Shadsworth Infant School (2018), available at: www.shadsworthinfants.co.uk/reception-1/

Standards and Testing Agency (2017), 'Early years foundation stage profile: 2018 handbook', available at: www.gov.uk/government/publications/early-years-foundation-stage-profile-2018-handbook

Tafuri, N. (2007), *The Busy Little Squirrel*. New York: Simon & Schuster.

Teaching Schools Council (2016), 'Effective primary teaching practice report 2016', avaiable at: https://www.tscouncil.org.uk/resources/effective-primary-teaching-practice-2016/

Wu, S. S., Chen, L., Battista, C., Smith Watts, A. K., Willcutt, E. G. and Menon, V. (2017), 'Distinct influences of affective and cognitive factors on children's non-verbal and verbal mathematical abilities', *Cognition*, 166, 118–129.

Index